# IN THE
# Military

Stories of experience, strength and hope from Grapevine

BOOKS PUBLISHED BY AA GRAPEVINE, INC.

*The Language of the Heart* (& eBook)
*The Best of the Grapevine Volume I* (& eBook)
*The Best of Bill* (& eBook)
*Thank You for Sharing*
*Spiritual Awakenings* (& eBook)
*I Am Responsible: The Hand of AA*
*The Home Group: Heartbeat of AA* (& eBook)
*Emotional Sobriety — The Next Frontier* (& eBook)
*Spiritual Awakenings II* (& eBook)
*In Our Own Words: Stories of Young AAs in Recovery* (& eBook)
*Beginners' Book* (& eBook)
*Voices of Long-Term Sobriety* (& eBook)
*A Rabbit Walks Into A Bar*
*Step by Step — Real AAs, Real Recovery* (& eBook)
*Emotional Sobriety II — The Next Frontier* (& eBook)
*Young & Sober* (& eBook)
*Into Action* (& eBook)
*Happy, Joyous & Free* (& eBook)
*One on One* (& eBook)
*No Matter What* (& eBook)
*Grapevine Daily Quote Book* (& eBook)
*Sober & Out* (& eBook)
*Forming True Partnerships* (& eBook)
*Our Twelve Traditions* (& eBook)
*Making Amends* (& eBook)
*Voices of Women in AA* (& eBook)

IN SPANISH
*El lenguaje del corazón*
*Lo mejor de Bill* (& eBook)
*El grupo base: Corazón de AA*
*Lo mejor de La Viña*
*Felices, alegres y libres* (& eBook)
*Un día a la vez* (& eBook)

IN FRENCH
*Le langage du coeur*
*Les meilleurs articles de Bill*
*Le Groupe d'attache: Le battement du coeur des AA*
*En tête à tête* (& eBook)
*Heureux, joyeux et libres* (& eBook)

# AA

## IN THE
## Military

Stories of experience, strength and hope from Grapevine

**AA**GRAPEVINE,Inc.

New York, New York

WWW. AAGRAPEVINE.ORG

Grapevine trademark, 1987

Copyright © 2018 by AA Grapevine, Inc.
475 Riverside Drive
New York, New York 10115
All rights reserved
May not be reprinted in full or in part, except in short passages for purposes
of review or comment, without written permission from the publisher.
AA and Alcoholics Anonymous are registered trademarks of AA World Services, Inc.
Twelve Steps copyright © AA World Services, Inc.; reprinted with permission
ISBN: 978-1-938413-63-6
Printed in Canada

# AA Preamble

Alcoholics Anonymous is a fellowship of men and women
who share their experience, strength and hope
with each other that they may solve their common problem
and help others to recover from alcoholism.

The only requirement for membership is a desire to stop drinking.
There are no dues or fees for AA membership;
we are self-supporting through our own contributions.
AA is not allied with any sect, denomination, politics, organization
or institution; does not wish to engage in any controversy,
neither endorses nor opposes any causes.

Our primary purpose is to stay sober
and help other alcoholics to achieve sobriety.

*© AA Grapevine, Inc.*

# Contents

CHAPTER TWO

## Air

*AA members who defend their country from the sky*

CHAPTER THREE

## Land

*Army, Marine and National Guard soldiers getting and staying sober*

CHAPTER FOUR

## Sea

*AA members who serve their country in the Navy or Coast Guard*

CHAPTER FIVE

## Over There

*AA members share about being stationed overseas, in faraway places, often at war*

CHAPTER SIX

## Women Serving Their Country

*Women soldiers share their experiences about getting and staying sober*

CHAPTER SEVEN

## Coming Home

*Experience, strength and hope from sober veterans*

# Welcome

---

"War fever ran high in the New England town to which
we new, young officers from Plattsburg were assigned."
Bill W., "Bill's Story," *Alcoholics Anonymous*

O*ur cofounder goes on to say that he grew lonely during his
military service in World War I and turned to alcohol, ignoring the "strong warnings" of "my people concerning drink."*

*To the many members of Alcoholics Anonymous who have served,
or are currently serving, in the military, Bill's words probably ring
familiar. Indeed, Bill's experiences are reflected in the many letters
that Grapevine has received from servicemen and women, from as far
back as 1944.*

*This book is a collection of 66 stories and letters, previously pub-
lished in Grapevine, by military AA members. In the first chapter,
early AA members recount their experiences staying sober or getting
sober while serving in faraway places and under high stress situations. As you'll read, Grapevine was often the sober lifeline that these
members depended on. Starting with the years around World War II,
something phenomenal happened. AA members took their programs
with them as they moved around the world—into the air, across the
land and under the sea, spreading the AA message and seeding groups
wherever they went.*

*Chapters 2, 3 and 4 are divided by area of service: Air (Air Force);
Land (Army, Marines and National Guard); and Sea (Navy and
Coast Guard). Chapter 5 chronicles the stories of AAs getting or staying sober in remote places across the globe, often during wartime,
where there was little, if any, contact with AA back home or even other
AAs in the service. Chapter 6 consists of stories by servicewomen, who
have served in many capacities, including in battle.*

*The final chapter, "Coming Home," is devoted to AA members who are veterans. Their stories frequently recount struggles with the emotional and physical aftermath of war experiences when they returned home. Their stories can be wrenching, with touches of AA-style humor. Their desire to try to give the gift of sobriety that they received to other veterans like themselves is inspiring.*

*This carrying of the AA message by our members in the military to faraway locales continues today. Groups continue to start up in remarkable places and harrowing situations, whether during a civil war in Mogadishu, Somalia (see "Incoming!" in Chapter 7) or a border crossing between Syria and Israel (see "Staying Sober in the Sand" in Chapter 5).*

*We salute our members who have served or are serving in the military. They give real meaning to carrying our message, often under difficult circumstances, to sick and suffering alcoholics everywhere.*

CHAPTER ONE

# Duty Called

The early days: Grapevine provides soldiers a vital connection
to AA during and after World War II

---

A lcoholics Anonymous was still a young Fellowship when World War II broke out. Hundreds of sober AA members in the United States and Canada would enter the armed forces, some with little sober time under their belts. They would be sent across North America and around the globe. This meant leaving behind friends and loved ones, hometowns and AA groups. Many in the Fellowship wondered how these members, with little or no access to meetings or other AAs, would be able to stay sober.

At this time, interest had already sparked in creating a newsletter with AA news and inspiration—and its potential value to our members in the military seemed enormous. This newsletter would become our beloved Grapevine, and for those in military service, their "meeting in print." From the very first issue, Grapevine kept servicemen and women connected to the Fellowship and our program of recovery, as the stories in this opening chapter attest.

In an article titled "Lieutenant Rediscovers the Beauties of Easy Does It" from 1944, M.L., a Second Lieutenant stationed in an "out-of-the-way place," Grapevine editors recognize "a cry for help." M.L. wrote of feeling a "total loss" when off duty and being unable to find "a single soul here that speaks the same language." After receiving her first issue of Grapevine, M.L. wrote in again: "Does that mean I'm to get it every month? It's proving no end of help to me."

Very early on, Grapevine also received letters from AAs struggling to adapt to the return to civilian life. In a department called "Mail Call for All AAs in the Armed Forces," published in the 1940s, a member writing with the initials T.D.Y. alerted AAs back home that "reconversion" from military to civilian life for AA members is "especially difficult—and dangerous." He also wrote "that application of the AA way of thinking will ease the transition for the veteran in many ways."

In a story called "Far From the Customary Skies," member R.H. of New York City wrote that he received his first issue of Grapevine in June of 1944. He was stationed overseas at the time and had only four months of sobriety. He wrote that he found "staying away from the first drink isn't easy." The arrival of Grapevine "changed all that for me," he added. He said that each issue that followed was "concrete evidence that we weren't forgotten."

The program helped these men and women get and stay sober far from home. And our servicemen and women helped carry our message across the globe and showed how to achieve sobriety in the most extreme circumstances.

## Points of View
August 1944

**D**ear Grapevine: Your thought for servicemen is excellent. Alcoholics are put to their greatest test while under stress. The emotions take over, and we are in great danger. The strain in the Army is terrific. Voices shouting orders, the hurry up and wait, arbitrary decisions which cause great inconvenience; these, and the whole idea of regimentation, create stress enough to knock us for several loops as things were in the old days. It was well expressed by the soldier who was asked by the Colonel's wife if he were happy in the service. "No, ma'am," he answered, "I'm nervous in the service." Then too, for those of us who like to be alone at times, it is extremely difficult. The only solitude I have been able to get in the Army has been in the middle of the drill field late at night.

Without the AA program I know that long before this I would have gotten into serious trouble. We must accept a situation we cannot change; and we learned in AA that the manner in which we accept things is infinitely more important than whatever we might have to accept. I don't recommend it as a cure, but I believe that this is a constructive, beneficial experience. I have been forced to depend upon AA to the utmost to remain as well as I have. Two slips in 20 months in the Army is, to me, an indication of what happens when we don't constantly practice our program.

*John D.*

## Lieutenant Rediscovers the Beauties of Easy Does It

*(From: Mail Call for All AAs in the Armed Forces)*
September 1944

One of the strongest motives behind the starting of the Grapevine—in fact the main thing that pushed the editors from the talking to the acting stage—was the need so often expressed in letters from AAs in the service for more AA news. We felt that their deep desire for a feeling of contact with AA might be fulfilled at least in part by such a publication—by us and for us. And, as the first issue emerged from the presses, a letter came to one of the editors from a woman AA, a Second Lieutenant stationed in an out-of-the-way place. It was a cry for help:

*... if things keep up the way they have been going I'm going to be in more trouble than I can handle. ... I've been recommended for promotion, but .... My work is more than satisfying, but off duty I'm a total loss. There isn't a single soul here that speaks the same language. ... The Army is a funny place. One is expected to drink, but not to get noisy or pass out or do any of the things drunks do. ... I've met a few AAs but we've only been in the same place for a short time. Several of them were in the same boat as I, skating on thin ice, but I don't know the outcome. Frankly, I'm scared. Has this problem been discussed at meetings? If so, has anyone offered any constructive suggestions?*

*M.L.*

A copy of the Grapevine went off by return mail. And now comes this:

*Dear Editors: The second copy of the Grapevine just arrived. Does that mean I'm to get it every month? It's proving no end of a help to me.*

*Thanks so much for getting it started, anyhow ... I guess there isn't much one can do about the sort of spot that I'm in. There isn't anything wrong but loneliness and boredom, and there's no way out of that, for now. ... Right after the first copy of the paper arrived I decided to try to take it a little easier (I'd forgotten all about 'Easy Does It'). ... I was working so very hard that the hectic on-duty and the static off-duty hours didn't mix. For some reason it doesn't seem as bad to be bored now.*

*P.S. I got that promotion I wrote you about.*

*M.L.*

## Far From the Customary Skies
June 1954

I received my first issue of the Grapevine (Vol. I, No. 1) in June of 1944. At that time I was in the Army, stationed overseas. So far as I knew then, there were no AAs within several thousand miles of me, so you can imagine the kick I got out of that first number.

There was more to it than that, of course. I think I probably felt a good deal like a shipwrecked sailor when the rescue vessel steams in sight. For what that first Grapevine did for me, more than anything else, was to assure me that I was not alone.

I had come into AA almost two years earlier, and through the miracle of this Fellowship found the sobriety I had been seeking. When I was drafted, after only four months in AA, I was secretly terrified I would start drinking again. Thanks to loyal AA friends who wrote me, and to the good God who brought me to AA, I didn't. But staying away from the first drink wasn't easy for me, and I lacked any real confidence that I would be able to make it stick.

Vol. I, No. 1 changed all that for me. Because after that I knew that no matter where I went, my Grapevine would sooner or later catch up with me. And I knew, too, that in its pages I would find the help I needed. Just knowing it was coming each month helped keep my defenses up. It was such a solid and reliable tie to AA-style sobriety (and no other style had ever worked for me!)

"Mail Call for All AAs in the Armed Forces" was especially helpful, for it was concrete evidence that we weren't forgotten. At the same time, it proved to me that others in the service were keeping the program ticking. To that extent, it made things easier for me.

Those days are long gone now, but Grapevine, happily, is still with us. I, for one, find it just as helpful now as it was in 1944. Today, it helps me in a different way—but none the less effectively. For one thing, I haven't gotten to meetings very frequently for the past year or so, and I find that Grapevine helps keep me from feeling out-of-touch. Not that Grapevine, or anything else, is a substitute for meetings, but it does help when you're not able to get around as much as you'd like.

One thing in particular I've always admired about Grapevine, and that is the readiness with which it has accepted "unorthodox" views. Such a reception is not always accorded the dissident elsewhere in AA.

I like the changes that have been made in Grapevine, too. Changes in format, changes in content, changes in personnel. Changes in almost everything, I expect, except in its basic purpose (Grapevine still dishes out my brand of AA). I understand they've even changed the financial picture—no more running in the red. For that accomplishment, a loud huzzah from this correspondent!

As you may gather from the foregoing, I am not one of those "old-timers" who yearn for the "good old days." I think both Grapevine—and AA—are better today than they ever were, for we have begun to mature

*R. H.*
*New York, New York*

## AA at Camp Peary

July 1944

**O**peration of the plan (Alcoholics Anonymous), at Camp Peary, an officer from the base declared at a big open meeting in Richmond, already has resulted in much good in its aid to officers in solving the problem of Navy men getting drunk on leave and overstaying their liberty. The AA group at the base, he said, occupy the same barracks and live with their problem, in close contact, seeking the solution among themselves.

This is part of a write-up of a semi-public meeting held in Richmond, Virginia on May 16th—the first meeting of its kind to be held there. Several ministers and physicians attended as special guests. Tom B. of New York and White Plains was the invited guest speaker. The article appeared in the Richmond Times-Dispatch, Wednesday, May 17, 1944.

## AA Is the Chaplain's Ally

June 1960

**T**his is the story of a small Alcoholics Anonymous group on an Air Force Base in Florida and what it was able to accomplish in the lives of men who were on their way out or in otherwise serious trouble in their military careers. In the short span of three years, 52 men in deep trouble over their drinking problems were restored to favor and acceptable duty. Some regained lost rank rapidly, and others by a slower route. Now most of them have not only new stripes as tangible evidence, but self-respect and family love to prove the value of a step which they should have taken long ago. It is the contention of this chaplain, who watched them progress from their great decision, that they might have taken the step sooner had the help been more readily available.

It is also his opinion that the formation of an AA group on any installation will prove to be a valuable ally in the chaplain program. Chaplains are involved in many consultations with families over the heartaches and contingent problems which result when the husband stays away from home or takes the family income for drink. We have seen too many broken homes where the only diagnosis is alcoholism. We could get at the root of these problems if we could convince men that AA can give the inspiration and help they need to overcome the major problem.

Why have a group on the military installation itself when an existing organization can usually be found in the neighboring community and is as close as the telephone? Too often the serviceman hesitates to join civilian groups lest his presence and his problem be a reflection upon his branch of the military service. To be with his own kind in a common endeavor to overcome a problem seems to make it an easier decision to reach.

It all started at our small base from the interest and initiative of "the old Sarge," as the organizer and leader of our group was affectionately called. His own story goes back to September 1950, when, at the age of 39, he stood before his commander in Panama a broken man mentally, physically and spiritually. He had been broken in rank all the way down to private. He was being handed dishonorable discharge papers as a chronic alcoholic, unfit for military service.

In his own words, Foster K. says, "I went back in memory at that very moment to my first tour of duty in Panama. When the Army transport docked at Pier 17 in Cristobal in December 1929, I looked out at a new world and dreamed of my future in the service. I was going to make something of myself. I wanted to complete my education and try for West Point. I fell in love with the service that morning. Everything—the officers in their white uniforms and their ladies wearing floral-patterned dresses and large straw hats, the Army band playing, troops marching off the transport—made me make this resolution." Then he came to himself to hear his commander say, "Just because you have failed in the service and must leave it doesn't mean that you should give up. You can still make a man of yourself. But you must get help for your drinking problem."

Foster K. doesn't know what prompted his reply. Perhaps it was the same locale 21 years later, and the realization that he had miserably failed his original resolution made there. But he said it: "Sir, I'll never take another drink as long as I live!" He believes it was not his doing. He was in no state to impress his Colonel with good intentions. He had said a silent prayer and believed it answered there in that office. His last request was that a member of AA meet him at the gate. The Colonel was impressed. He tore up the papers, restored Foster K. to duty, and arranged for his family to join him there.

Six years later, the old Sarge wrote a letter to the colonel to let him know that he had remained sober—a day at a time—and informed him that in October 1956 he had received his certificate for permanent master sergeant. I saw the Colonel's answer to that letter: "I cannot overstate my pleasure upon learning of your success. ... One of the most difficult problems a commander faces is that of making decisions which may have a permanent impact upon a man's career. ... I am proud to have had a small part in helping you change your approach to life, and I wish you every continued success."

M/Sgt. Foster K. and S/Sgt. Sandy Z. and two members from a civilian group met in the chaplain's office in February 1956 to organize the base group. From that small beginning the organization grew. Visits were made to commanders and first sergeants to explain the program. A favorable reaction on the part of many who earnestly wanted to help their men with this problem added impetus. The growth was materially aided also by a discerning base commander who let his policy be known through his staff that "no stigma whatsoever will be placed upon any airman or officer who seeks help through the group."

It wasn't long until the base began to take notice through the change taking place in the new members. Jim W., Ken S., Phil W., Gene R., Russell N., Aubry C., and many others had a testimony to give to others in their outfits as to what AA was doing for them. The first annual meeting brought an attendance of 150 from the base group and well-wishers, and from the neighboring civilian groups who wanted to lend their support to the program on base. After getting started in their own group, military members found it easier and helpful to attend meetings off base. By this time, many had spoken before civilian groups along the Florida coast and some had attended the state convention. In the struggle with the same problem, a genuine link had come between the military and these civilians from all walks of life.

I could not begin to tell the story of all who gained sobriety and regained self-respect and the esteem of the service. Perhaps the best way to show my conviction that AA is the best avenue to help a man whose basic problem is alcohol is to tell of two among those I have helped to find their solution in AA. (The most satisfying commendation I have ever received came from a leader of our group who spoke of me once as "the silent partner.")

With the telling of these brief histories, I hope my conviction will be evident that this is not only tremendously worth the chaplain's time but worth the time and effort of the military service as well. It costs thousands of dollars to recruit and train a replacement for the alcoholic who gets kicked out. It costs a great deal to rehabilitate a prisoner who has broken the law or violated the military code of justice. There is a huge investment to restore to duty the injured and ill. It costs only a few cups of coffee and time spent at meetings to reclaim a man whose sickness is alcohol. True, not all can be reclaimed, and some who start out on the program fail. But to make the program available on the installation, even closer than an off-base telephone number, is to point the way to possible retention of good men whose only failing is the bottle.

Like the old Sarge himself, Andy was on his way out when he came to my office on the fourth of April 1957. Here is the picture: Take an airman with almost 18 years' service, 13 as master sergeant, married, with four children. Now reduce him to basic airman, add a couple of court-martials, and tell him if he gets drunk again he will be discharged under other than honorable conditions. Give him an alcoholic wife, bad checks out against him, and heavy indebtedness. Put him on K.P. sick with a hangover, broke, disgusted with himself, and almost ready to give up. He comes rather reluctantly into the chaplain's office—almost as if this is the last straw.

You can imagine that it would take a lot of convincing to get him to see that it is possible for him to do something about his plight. He still doesn't admit he is an alcoholic, but he finally agrees to give it a try. It takes almost as much convincing for his commander to give him the chance. Finally, it is agreed. Andy and his wife go to the AA meeting on base. They keep going. They go to meetings in two communities as many as four times in one week. He begins to straighten up. Much of the credit goes to his wife, Lucile, who believes in the program and encourages him to continue.

Finally, after several weeks, he gets enough courage to speak at a meeting. For a rough-and-ready, hard-fighting, hard-drinking, six-foot Texan to get up and say, "My name is Andy, and I am an alcoholic," and to admit that he is powerless over alcohol and would go to any lengths to overcome it, is almost a miracle. From then on Andy was a talked-about airman. From April to November his progress was marked from disgrace to airman-of-the-month and rewarded with stripes from basic airman to staff sergeant. I was present when the squadron promotion board skipped airman first class to make him a noncommissioned officer again.

The other member for whom it meant holding back other than honorable discharge papers introduced himself at meetings by saying, "My name is Eric K. I am an alcoholic and an Eskimo." Shy, confused, lost in a society he had only recently joined, Eric K. had found sociability in drinking. From high school in Alaska into the Air Force and what was "foreign service" for him down in Florida, Eric had drifted into more and more drinking. He was a risk down on the line, of possible danger not only to himself but to a crew taking off in an aircraft which might have a maintenance error under the wrench-wielding of one so undependable.

Eric K. justified the 90-day extension period granted him to prove himself by staying sober. Word of his AA activity was reported weekly to his commander. He was put back with his maintenance crew. He began to attend church regularly under the emphasis of AA upon spiritual help. The group helped him to overcome his shyness and the feeling of being an outsider in the realization that this had been a basic factor in his drinking. Eric K. is an accepted military serviceman today.

To recognize an alcoholic is not very difficult for most chaplains. The pattern has been pretty well established. If the chaplain can help a man to face the facts and admit that outside help is necessary, he will lead the man to the only hope there is.

The little group in this account was disbanded when the base closed. But it is now worldwide in its outreach. Sandy Z. went to a Midwestern base to continue his activities. Ken S. and his wife started a group in France, where the last report tells of nine airmen joining AA through their efforts. Andy has helped six men to find sobriety in the Philippines. The old Sarge retired from military service with honors and continues his work through community groups. The story of these and others may never end. But they are remaining sober—24 hours at a time. We ought to think soberly about making this help available to others.

*Spencer D. McQueen*

# Mail Call for All AAs in the Armed Forces
March 1945

I t is becoming increasingly apparent that AA is going to be called upon to perform a real job in aiding many veterans of this war during or, more particularly, some time after their reentry into civilian life. We believe, therefore, that the following piece, written for Grapevine by an AA who is himself in the process of undergoing this readjustment, following Army experiences that included participation in the invasion of Normandy, is extremely timely.

*-The Editors*

Becoming acclimated to a tailless shirt—assuming you can find any at all—is a small but symbolic problem that every veteran of the military forces encounters in making the transition to civilian ways of life.

The tailless shirt is not the only reason for feeling shorn. The veteran also feels that a number of other things besides the tail of his shirt are missing. The Army—or the Navy, or whatever his branch of the service—is no longer taking care of him. The privileges and protection that the uniform provides, along with the responsibilities, have come to an end. Your assignment, whatever it may have been, has been finished. There's no longer somebody on hand to tell you, whether you were officer, soldier or sailor, what to do next. You can't even get cigarettes when you want them. You're just another short-tailed civilian, mister!

The dischargee not only misses the things he found enjoyable while wearing a uniform. Strangely, he also misses some of the things he disliked the most. He may yearn for the very things that used to draw his loudest and longest gripes. If he happens to be a veteran from a combat zone, he may even miss some of the gadgets and conditions that scared him silly while he was in the middle of them. When, for instance, in New York he hears the weekly Saturday noon air raid sirens and, after an involuntary tightening of nerves, he remembers that they're only practice, he may wish momentarily (only momentarily) that they were the real thing. It's not that he ever liked robots or enemy raiders; it's that his nerves are still attuned to the excitement and tension that a combat zone produces in generous quantities as a daily and nightly fare. War in one phase or another has been reality to him. That has now been removed and what's left seems, at times, unreal and even empty.

Another void becomes apparent in topics of conversation in normal circles. What the veteran has been talking about morning, noon and night for however long he has been in uniform is scarcely suitable now. People just aren't interested in what Sgt. Doakes said to Capt. Whoozit. And you certainly can't blame them for that. Even when they are genuinely interested in hearing something of his experiences, the dischargee discovers that there's a great deal he can't express in a way that is understandable to someone who has not felt what he has.

So he tends to avoid the subject—and he certainly does avoid it after one or two encounters with the occasional person who reacts to war anecdotes with a look in his eye that says, "What a line this guy's got!" In such cases, the dischargee learns that what may be commonplace in theaters of war may sound fantastic and unbelievable elsewhere.

All of these factors add up to an emotional disturbance involving lonesomeness, injured vanity, loss of poise and direction, fear of the future and resentments. For many persons, of course, relief at being permitted to return to normal pursuits offsets the other factors. But reconversion from the military to the civilian world calls for considerable readjustments for anyone. For an AA member, the readjustment may be especially difficult—and dangerous.

Paradoxically, an AA who has had no or little trouble during his enforced separation from the group may be in greater danger during this period of readjustment than the one who has had an up and down fight all the way from enlistment or induction to discharge. If he has gone through military service without any slips or near-slips he has scored a real achievement. The military life imposes severe handicaps on an AA. It usually prevents him from practicing many of the steps on which he normally depends. It divorces him from group therapy, 12th Step work and inspirational talks. It precipitates him into circumstances that are upsetting and that tend to unbalance anyone's sense of values.

If the AA has survived all of that successfully, he's likely to feel pretty strong when he returns to normal life. Certainly he feels that now, once again within his home orbit, among AA friends and within reach of all the help he could ask for, he is in much less danger, alcoholically, than he was in the service away from home. So he may very easily let down. He may drop his guard. He may become "too tired" to attend any meetings or do any 12th Step work. He may slack off in doing some of the little things that help to keep an AA growing along AA lines.

If he begins to slide off in any of these ways, he's heading for a tailspin and a tight inside loop. Whatever hazardous tendencies he may develop will be aggravated by the emotional disturbances which his military-to-civilian readjustment is bound to create for him even if he remains squarely on the beam. The fact is, he has need to double his guard and keep his defenses on the alert during this period.

Those are facts which this AA had to learn the painful way. But in learning those, he also learned that application of the AA way of thinking will ease the transition for the veteran in many ways. Again I have seen how AA not only helps to overcome Personal Enemy No. 1, but how infinitely effective it is on many other human problems.

Again too, I have been reminded forcefully that in AA one cannot stand still for long—he either goes backwards or he grows, and he grows only by using a gradually increasing amount of AA.

*T.D.Y.*

## Guam Calling
May 1948

We hanker for Stateside voices, and Stateside letters is the plea to AA Grapevine from Guam. It is pretty lonesome out here, so some letters or recordings would be greatly appreciated by the group on the island. The islanders promise prompt reply to anyone caring to write. Letters may be sent to: M.K.K., c/o USED, Station 15, Guam, Guam.

*Guam*

## Report From Okinawa
June 1953

Okinawa! To most people that is a word more or less un-known and to some, a reminder of war-torn days in the Far Pacific. But to 100 or so now happy men and women it brings but one quick thought: That's where I found AA.

These people are now reassigned to various other remote spots on the globe, in construction camps, war zones or military installations, and some are even in the good old U.S.A. To all of them the Pioneer Group on Okinawa sends greetings and best wishes for the continuation of the good work they started or carried on while here.

A civil engineer from Florida, Woody W., got the group going here about six years ago and is still here, proving a solid inspiration for all of us in the group and giving unstintingly of his time and experiences in order to carry the message to any alcoholic who shows the least desire to do something about his own problem.

Due to rotation of military personnel and short-term contracts for civilians there is a heavier-than-normal turnover in our membership, but the size of the group remains fairly constant as new members come in at about the same rate that members are rotated home.

Grapevine has provided us with much food for thought; nearly every meeting includes subjects for discussion or quotes from one of the copies. We look forward to every issue with keen anticipation.

As each member's time draws near he begins checking up in the AA Directory to locate the group nearest to his home or new duty station. This is a good sign that he has found the AA way of life to be the solution to his problem and that he has hope in his heart for continued sobriety and peace of mind.

If a member from Okinawa shows up in your home group, please give him an extra-warm handclasp for us and let him know that our thoughts and prayers are for him.

*Bob S.*
*Okinawa*


# AA Air-Borne

*(From: From the Grass Roots)*
May 1959

I am a member of the RCAF and was one of the last few to leave Claresholm, Alberta, after the closing of the RCAF Station there.

The Air Base officially closed in August 1958, but my wife and

I did not get out of Claresholm until December 17. During this period there were numerous "closing out" parties going on and an awful temptation to drink. It was only through God's help and the kind understanding and capable assistance of AA friends in Fort MacLeod, Lethbridge, and Picture Butte and having AA Grapevine handy that I was able to stay sober.

I am now stationed in Calgary and approaching my second year of sobriety with AA. I wouldn't trade any part of the sober time for any part of my life when I was drinking. It took three slips before I finally stuck with AA and the last time I came in without reservations and with an honest admission that I am an alcoholic.

I am only 24 now and sure hope that other young people can find AA as soon in life as I did and save themselves a lot of misery that drinking can bring. Both my wife and I really enjoy the new way of life we have found with AA. We enjoy reading Grapevine every month and hope you keep up the good work.

*J.M.*
*Calgary, Alberta*

## A Flier Lands

*(From: Mail Call for All AAs at Home or Abroad)*
January 1947

It was an unexpected pleasure to receive your very nice letter. I suppose the explanation as to why I finally joined AA is now in order, so here goes. My glittering career in the Army was studded with several meteoric rises and just as rapid falls. I went from a private to technical sergeant twice before they finally made me a flight officer. I managed to hold onto that for a little longer period than the others, but even that wound up when I went on a ferry trip and landed the ship at the wrong base, so cockeyed I couldn't walk away from it. I might have gotten away with that if I hadn't gotten my copilot drunk too. This last little episode was really the whizzer of them all. I was transferred to a new base and became the only flying private in the Air Corps.

Things went so well they decided to start me up the ladder again; so they gave me a little rank. (This was in January, 1945.) Naturally I had to celebrate it, so I went to town for two quarts and wound up in Kansas City, Missouri (60 miles away). It was such a fine place and the people so hospitable that I lengthened my stay to 60 days. On the 60th day they came after me! The rest is history! I drew a sentence of three years at hard labor, which I very rightly deserved.

It was while I was at Jefferson Barracks that a group of us decided to try and start AA in the Disciplinary Barracks. It really worked out much better than we had hoped. When we moved down here we really went to work in such earnest, in fact, that a few of us are in for parole to the AA group in Louisville, and jobs are waiting there for us. I have made several speeches before the Louisville group, which is some 300 persons, and all in all have really come out of the fog for the first time. I hate to admit it, but these people did me a favor when they locked me up.

*H. R.*
*Fort Knox, Kentucky*

CHAPTER TWO

# Air

### AA members who defend their country from the sky

This chapter is a collection of stories by AA members who entered Air Forces in the United States or Canada. Some entered the military already sober—and quickly realized the new lengths they would have to go to stay that way. For many, their drinking escalated once in the service. When they tried to seek help, some encountered a military culture with little tolerance for alcoholics, although more recent stories suggest this is changing.

In the story, "A Tiger Is Tamed," member D.R., a Louisiana farm boy with "flying fever," joins the Army Air Force on his 18th birthday in 1942. Later, in a tour of duty during the Korean War, D.R. fulfills a dream to fly F-84s (delivering A-bombs). On one test flight, however, he describes himself as "too drunk to walk properly." Such incidents, he writes, were "getting uglier." After quitting the military, he goes to his first AA meeting, where he meets "a dozen alcoholics just like me."

In the story, "Uniformed Recovery," Leo R. of Portsmouth, Virginia finds AA in 1957 while on active duty in the U.S. Air Force. He describes some in the military as having a "dim view of us," meaning alcoholics, whether sober or drinking. Indeed, the meeting he helped start had to move off base. But he paints a different picture several years later when he visits that same meeting, finding Air Force personnel in uniform—and it "did not seem to matter what one's rank was."

Bob B. of Puyallup, Washington writes in his story, "Learning to Fly," how he came into AA "a beaten former Air Force command pilot." He likens his discovery of our Fellowship and Twelve Steps to "finally landing a battered aircraft, crippled from a long combat *mission, shot full of bullet holes, on its last engine, fuel tank filled with nothing but fumes."*

*In 1983's "Pull the Rip Cord," member C.K. of Fort Benning, Georgia writes that he's 18 years old and has been in the program for over two years. He says that he has experienced many things that would not have happened "if I were still drinking." In airborne school, he made five jumps in his last week and felt "the presence of my Higher Power."*

## Learning to Fly

August 2011

I came into AA over a decade ago, a beaten former Air Force command pilot. After I retired from active duty, years of excessive alcohol consumption took me on a long flight from reality to a destination of desperation and despair. My final alcoholic days landed me flat on my back in a detox treatment center. Discovering AA and the Twelve Steps was like finally landing a battered aircraft, crippled from a long combat mission, shot full of bullet holes, on its last engine, fuel tank filled with nothing but fumes. I couldn't have flown another minute, or walked another alcoholic mile, if I hadn't landed safely in the hospital.

It took a few days in detox before I started to feel like I might be on the mend, realizing gradually that recovery wasn't going to be easy or quick. There was no supersonic cure available for this old pilot. I'd been flying on gin and vermouth for more years than I cared to remember, and it was going to take time, treatment and trained experts to get me back to quality flying condition.

In my 25 years as a USAF pilot, I held IP (Instructor Pilot) ratings in three different airplanes. My job was to teach pilots how to fly these three specific military aircraft, each one complex and unique. Flying complicated airplanes skillfully is very much like soberly facing the difficult challenges of life. In flying, you need to study books on theories and procedures, but to succeed you need to get in the cockpit, put your hands on the controls and practice. The Air Force taught me that repetition is the key to learning to fly. Each complex flying task is done over and over until you get it right. Recovery from alcohol addiction is the same. First, you study the Big Book, learn the Steps, then practice what you've learned until it becomes second nature. Practice, practice, practice.

You don't become a great chef just by reading cookbooks. You can start with books of course, but at some point you'll have to get in the kitchen and turn on the stove. This goes for artists, musicians, athletes and anyone else who wants to be really good at something. You'll need to practice every chance you get. Successful sober living takes practice as well.

Early on, I realized that my mission objective wasn't just to stop drinking, although that was part of it, but to learn how to live life sober again. Today, I'm convinced there's a difference. Just stopping the consumption of booze won't do it. My practice today involves daily meetings, joining a home group and getting involved as a trusted servant. It's nothing magical or miraculous but so far, with practice, it's worked.

The Big Book is my "flight manual" that guides my life and sets a standard for daily behavior. I found a sponsor who would be my instructor, not only to make sure I learned the essentials (the Twelve Steps, for instance) but to dissuade me from making serious mistakes that could ultimately cause me to spin, crash and burn.

When I first came into AA and I heard people announce that they had 10 or 20 years in sobriety, I simply couldn't believe it. If they were recovered for that long, why would they keep coming back to meetings? Then it occurred to me that as a pilot, even when I had thousands of flying hours under my belt, I still had to practice the basics, making sure I stayed current with the regulations and evaluating my progress at regular intervals.

After over 13 years of sobriety, I've truly found a new freedom in AA and I'll be forever grateful. I still learn something new almost daily. I don't fly military airplanes anymore, but AA has given me the ability to skillfully navigate the skies of this sober life.

*Bob B.*
*Puyallup, Washington*

# Uniformed Recovery

May 2005

I found AA and sobriety in 1957, while on active duty in the United States Air Force at Kessler AFB, Mississippi. My sponsor was first sergeant of one of the Air Base Groups. The AA group we attended was in Gulfport, the only AA group between Mobile, Alabama, and New Orleans. There were many military people in the group, ranging from airman to brigadier general. I know that my sponsor, Woody, was instrumental in getting groups started in Newfoundland, Clark Field in the Philippines, Warner Robins AFB, Georgia, and Forbes AFB in Topeka, Kansas.

In 1965, I transferred to a NATO standby base in Chaumont, France. In order to attend meetings I had to travel to Metz, which was the headquarters for the Canadian Air Force in Europe. Sometimes I drove two hours each way to attend the meeting in Zwibruken, Germany, which was another Canadian AFB. They were good meetings, and the Canadians were always glad to have visitors. There was one army master sergeant named Joe who drove about 75 miles, and I would drive about the same distance and we would meet in the library of an Air Force supply depot. We did this for about two years and only one other guy ever showed up. His name was George. He had been reduced in grade and was about to get kicked out of the Air Force. They gave him a second chance and at the last contact I had with George, he had regained his position and was technical sergeant.

I am not too sure of the year, but I pitched my tent and camped along the Rhine River outside of Wiesbaden, Germany, and attended the European Roundup. This was really an all-European gathering, but it was run—or managed—by AAs in the American military and held at the Hap Arnold High School on the air base. The following year, they turned the entire Roundup over to the German AA members, who conducted the Roundup in the Swartzerbach Hotel in Wiesbaden. Both were wonderful experiences of AA cooperation and togetherness.

I made a journey to Berlin and stayed on Tempelhof AFB during a convention. I was unable to locate any AA members on that air base and had no German contacts. I went into the NCO club for lunch and sat alone and prayed that I could make a contact. Not two minutes later, an Air Force master sergeant who had been a member of my home group in Gulfport, Mississippi, walked into the dining room. Jim was a real blessing. We had lunch together. The interesting thing was that Jim was not stationed there. He was a crew member of an Air Force plane just stopping for refueling.

After returning to the States, I was stationed at Scott AFB, Illinois, where we managed to get a meeting started on the base. In those days some military folks had a dim view of us admitting that we were alcoholic. We were actually forced to move the meeting off base. A small church gave us a place to meet. They were surprised when we insisted on paying rent. The three years at Scott were really good years. I completed college while there and made progress in my military career. I retired from the USAF in 1970. I had the opportunity to visit Scott AFB some years later and was pleased to see that they not only had AA meetings on base, but Al-Anon also. People attended meetings in uniform, but it did not seem to matter what one's rank was. Some of them were on duty at the time of the meeting and they were able to be relieved of their duty long enough to attend.

My home group includes several military, both active duty and retired. They lend a great deal to the group and they willingly share their experience, strength and hope.

Fast-forward to 2004. I am working for the United States Navy as a counselor in an alcohol and drug rehabilitation facility. I still have contact with branches of the military stationed all over the world. These are great people and good AA members. They carry the message wherever they go. Many of the local retired members return to our facility to share their experience, strength and hope with the active duty, retired and civilian dependents who are treated at this facility. I am a happy member of AA and proud to have shared this journey with the men and women of the armed forces.

*Leo R.*
*Portsmouth, Virginia*

## Pull the Rip Cord

*(From: Dear Grapevine)*
May 1983

'm 18 years old and have been in the program for over two years now. At this time, I am in the Army.

When I was in my last week of airborne school, I made five jumps. It was during my jumps that I really felt the presence of my Higher Power, whom I consider to be God.

When I was drinking, I was in constant free-fall, not caring what was in my way. I did eventually find this program, and it was then that my canopy opened. I finally realized what was happening to me. It was in AA that I learned how to be me, to face the world sober for a change.

Since I've been in the program, many things have happened to me that I believe wouldn't have happened if I were still drinking. I graduated high school, and went through 13 weeks of infantry training and three weeks of airborne school. But most of all, I saw myself grow up.

When times get tough, just remember to pull the rip cord, and your chute will be there.

*C. K.*
*Fort Benning, Georgia*

## A Tiger Is Tamed
February 1970

I grew up in North Louisiana, first on a farm in a small town, then in a moderate-sized town, then in a city. After I had worked my way through high school and one year of college, I got flying fever and joined the Army Air Force on my 18th birthday, in 1942. I breezed through flying school in good shape, graduating as a second lieutenant in October 1943. My assignment to fighters fulfilled my fondest aspirations, and early in 1944 I went to China, where I flew the shark-nosed P-40s of Chennault's Flying Tigers. This was my cup of tea; I loved to fly, and a fighter pilot in China came about as near as possible to being his own man. I liked it well enough to volunteer for a second tour of combat, but to my disgust the war ended just as I got back to China.

After thinking it over, I accepted a reserve commission and set out to finish college. Thanks to the Veterans Administration and a facile intelligence, for which I take no credit, I managed to graduate on schedule. I immediately rejoined the Air Force, telling myself it was because I loved to fly. In retrospect, I think maybe it had more to do with the uniform, the ribbons, and the rank. A year later, I met and married a girl I considered truly unique, and for once I was right.

Very quickly, I was fighting in Korea. I survived, though narrowly, and broke into jets after my return. I also broke into an outfit that possessed a fine bunch of pilots. I had hardly gotten qualified in the F-84 when we were handed the top-secret mission of carrying and delivering A-bombs, the first fighter outfit assigned to do so. After a crash program of training and equipping, we moved to England to reduce the temperature of the Cold War. We were there more than three years.

My drinking had begun in China, progressed sporadically until my senior year in college, and then settled down to a daily routine. It was easy to drink in England, and the good times were plentiful. Needless to say, I had no inkling that my behavior pattern was abnormal; but even then there were incidents that were less than creditable to an officer and a gentleman. I once test-hopped an F-84 when I was too drunk to walk properly, an insane performance in which I took considerable pride at the time. The occasions when I flew with varying loads aboard were too numerous to detail, and if I ever complied with the Air Force regulation forbidding flying within 24 hours after drinking, it was accidental. There was no overt notice taken of my peccadilloes, but there was a mysterious development in my career that I never could explain: I applied twice for a Regular Air Force commission, and was rejected.

I had pretty well missed the boat for a successful military career. Things were piling up on me; the "incidents" were getting uglier and the happy times scarcer. I quit the service, less than six years from retirement age, and started at the bottom as an oil-field service engineer.

For a while, it seemed that the combination of a new career and a geographical change had solved all my problems. I liked the work and took great pride in the prestige of my company. I started off like a ball of fire, despite being a little old for a beginner in that line, but all too soon the world started picking on me again. The money was pretty good, but it took all there was and a little more to keep me in martinis and vodka (the latter to carry in my car, in the happy delusion that it was undetectable).

I transferred to offshore work, which meant more money, but also long stretches in the Gulf of Mexico, far from my sources of supply. Even with the enforced abstinence on the job, my increased income failed to keep up with my thirst. After a year or so, I was desperate, and I applied for a transfer to Canada. Not as a cure for my drinking, mind you; I just needed a new challenge! I made it to Rock Springs, Wyoming, instead, and once again the geographical cure seemed to work magic. My wife and kids liked the new, big country, and the work was different enough to divert me from drinking for appreciable spells.

But inevitably, the monstrous spiral tightened. The joys faded out of my life, my debts began to mount, my boss's tolerance was wearing thin, and my wife actually had the gall to tell me it was all because of my drinking! She had plenty of reason to leave me, but there was never enough money to get her out of town. Worst of all was my mental condition. All motivation had vanished, except the desperate urge to drink.

I knew by now that I was drinking too much, but I also knew I couldn't cut down, because I had tried it, using all the pitiful little schemes. I wasn't willing even to consider cutting it out entirely; I couldn't visualize living without drinking. I had tried that too, for a month or so, and had been utterly miserable the whole time. Whatever affection I had for my wife and family was totally immolated in my frantic pursuit of alcohol. My job and my company were meaningless to me except as a necessary source of drinking money.

Finally, one January day in 1965, I stopped my car on a snowy hillside just outside the town, and thought. I wasn't sober; in fact, I hadn't been sober for more than a year, but I was perhaps more lucid than usual.

The things I thought about were not pleasant. I sought a reason, just one solitary reason, why I ought to go on home. I couldn't think of one. I knew there was no hope of finding pleasure or satisfaction or gratitude or even mere comfort anywhere. There was simply no hope. I could not remember the last happy moment I had experienced, but I knew it was a long time gone. My thoughts turned, as they had many times before, toward the one alternative to continued torment. I had pretty well settled on bashing in the muffler on my car, in such a way as to vent the exhaust inside, and then simply going to sleep. This plan attracted me because it was painless, fairly certain, and not too obviously suicide. It was not unusual for me to sleep in the car, and there was always the chance that a rock could have damaged the muffler by accident. I didn't really give much of a damn what anybody thought, but the faint vestige of a conscience I had left urged me to spare my family the disgrace.

Somehow another idea crept into my mind: Why not give the medics a chance? I had no real hope that they could help; my case was obviously like no other. Still, it wouldn't hurt to try.

Well, I tried. By the grace of God, the doctor I went to sent me to AA, and by that time I was too limp to resist. To my surprise, I met a dozen alcoholics just like me, only soberer, and I read about hundreds more in the AA literature. After fighting it off through a long, nasty slip, I finally got it through my head that I was just a member of the human race, and not such a hot one at that.

I'm not out of the woods entirely; even now, I sit here thinking what a crackerjack piece this is, and how impressed everybody will be when you print it. My motive is not merely to see my immortal words in print, though that may enter in. Part of it is simply my need to put my feelings into words, to remind myself once more how close I am, and always will be, to utter ruin. And maybe a little of it is genuine hope that my very typical story will make the way easier for someone else.

*D. R.*
*Rock Springs, Wyoming*

## In Defense of "Special Groups"
*(From: Dear Grapevine)*
October 1982

A special-interest group for gay men and women is an AA meeting; members discuss their alcoholism. I feel more comfortable at a meeting where I know there isn't going to be any prejudice or judgment about my sexuality. At an AA meeting for gays, confused newcomers are able to deal with their alcoholism assisted by their peers, not feeling they have to hide a major portion of their lives at the same time.

I got sober while in the Air Force. This was the beginning of my own self-acceptance as a whole person. Today, I'm able to "come out" at all meetings when I speak, but I don't know if I would be sober without the gay meetings as a supplement to regular AA.

*C. D.*

*Danbury, Connecticut*

# Battle of the Bottle
July 1951

Oakland, California's Group 20 brought into being and nurtured into full bloom by our beloved "Jim" and his lovely wife Ruth, started the evening with the usual moment of silence. Eddie was chairman and Steps Eight and Nine were to be discussed—making amends.

There were so many present that it was impossible for Eddie to get around to all. Had he called on me I would have attempted to relate the following little story.

Army Air Corps, 1942. Plans, formulated by brilliant military minds, were now being put into action in order to knock the German Luftwaffe out of the skies. I was doing my part—in spurts. Working long hours for a month or two and then falling apart, struggling to pull myself together again in an attempt to be the right kind of a G.I. I continued to fight the battle of the bottle but made little impression on the enemy. Through much effort during sober periods I became an important cog in our Command Headquarters. My Colonel, a battle-scarred old-timer dating back to World War I, relied on me to the extent that when I laid a sheaf of papers upon his desk for signature he usually signed them without delay. He, in fact, took me under his wing. It seems like yesterday that when I'd take five drunken days to get back from a three day pass, he'd order the guardhouse gates opened up for my release, and tell me to clean up and report back for duty. The boys around the base thought up a little tune referring to my delay in getting back on time: "Billy, won't you please come home?"

Following these episodes there would be a fairly long period of sobri-ety and hard work, many trips into the Colonel's office loaded down with perfectly executed orders, reports, memoranda, etc. for his signature.

The Colonel was a grizzled and rough old-timer, affectionately called "The Bull of the Woods" when he wasn't within hearing dis-tance. Impatient and curt with Majors and Captains, he was very pa-tient with me, with the exception of his occasional bellowing when I slipped off the deep end. Somehow that officer must have known that I was fighting a terrific battle—the battle of alcoholism wherein no well-laid plan of mine brought victory. His advice to me was: "Soldier, most of us like a few drinks now and then. No harm in that. But re-member to handle your liquor like a soldier!"

An eminent psychiatrist, one of two nationally famous brothers in that field, had been called to active duty and one day visited our Air Base. A sober and hardworking Bill (on that particular day) was instructed to report to the hospital. Following an hour-long private audience with the doc, he told me that I was an alcoholic. So long as I'd leave liquor entirely alone, I was a definite asset to the service, but only under that condition. Later I told my Colonel about that au-dience and he bellowed: "Those brain busters are nuts. Don't know what's getting into this Army. You are on the beam so stay that way."

But my periodic battle of the bottle continued. One day my Colonel took off in a B-17 never to return. The only consolation I could then find was in the fact that at least most of the time I was putting out good work and thereby eased to some degree the terrific burden he was car-rying on his shoulders as the Executive Officer of a large Command.

Colonel, wherever you now are, stationed with other old soldiers who have successfully completed their missions on this earth, I hope that you can look down upon this AA meeting and have the satisfac-tion of knowing that there is a successful battle plan to conquer man's ancient enemy—alcohol. It is a simple plan. You see it in operation right now. We must admit that you and I were wrong in the strategy of my "having a few drinks and handling it like a soldier." We must concede that the psychiatrist was right—but he offered no plan for victory. His "don't drink" advice would be like the General telling you to go out and kill off all the enemy and then we'd win the war.

It may be my imagination, but it seems that I can hear that old gruff voice of yours right now: "OK soldier, you've been briefed. Your plane is the one with that AA banner emblazoned on her nose. Finest crew on earth will be flying with you. Keep her on course. Remain constantly on the alert for approaching enemy aircraft—resentments, fears, jealousies, indecisions, and the rest of those devils who will do their best to sneak up on you.

"When your mission is accomplished and your craft is headed out to sea toward the setting sun, remember soldier, I'll be standing by to watch you come in. Good flying, boy ... and here's to a happy landing!"

Thanks Colonel, for your understanding—then and now.

*B. B.*
*Oakland, California*

## AA in a New Town
September 2006

After almost 15 years in the Air Force as an enlisted man, I was called into my first sergeant's office and asked if I had a problem with alcohol. I explained why I drank a bit more than other people: my wife wouldn't follow me to my new duty station; I now lived in dormitories filled with young airmen; my car was an old wreck; I had little money available, and what I had seemed to disappear each month.

With patience and understanding, the sergeant and my commander went over my record and explained the disease of alcoholism. It was the first time I really reviewed my life and saw that alcohol might have something to do with my situation. Within a couple of hours, I concluded that I might be an alcoholic. Later that evening, I attended my first AA meeting and have not stopped going since.

I attended meetings three times a day, which my squadron leadership supported. I lived, breathed, and thought of one thing: staying sober. I got a sponsor who guided me through the Steps and showed me how to stay sober for today. When I was a few days sober, my sponsor's sponsor's sponsor came into the noon meeting in a motorized chair. My sponsor asked me to get him a cup of coffee. I did, and started a ritual of giving service to a member. With nine years in the program, my greatest joy is still getting a man a cup of coffee.

With 32 days of sobriety, the military decided that two weeks in a treatment center would do me some good. I disagreed, but thankfully they didn't listen to my objections. My sponsor and I talked several times about going to meetings outside the area when I went on leave and temporary duty to several places around the world. My sponsor made it clear that when traveling, I shouldn't try to change AA in a community. "Listen and share your experience, strength and hope," he said, "but don't give advice."

About a year before I got sober, my wife decided not to move when I received a new assignment in the South. My three young boys stayed with their mother. I moved on to a new assignment with lots of dreams and a bad drinking problem that I could not see. Until I did my Fifth Step, I would not admit it was the best decision she could have made at the time.

Soon after getting sober, and several times during the next five years, I tried to convince my soon-to-be-ex-wife to move with our kids to the city where I now lived.

My eldest son moved in with me when I was three years sober, and I started learning how to be a dad to a teenager. He was 14 and immediately flourished in Alateen. When my son worked his program and attended conferences, it gave my program an even bigger boost. I offered everything I could to my ex-wife to move with the children, but she refused. After talking with my sponsor and some close friends, I decided I needed to reunite my three boys, regardless of how much I loved the city, the meetings and the people of the South. It was not about my comfort zone, it was about my responsibilities. In order to stay true to myself and my AA program, I moved to Plattsburgh, New York, where my boys lived.

With the help of my squadron, home group, sponsor, AA and the dear friends that God had put in my path, I retired from the military with three things: a little over 20 years of military service, an extra stripe on my sleeve and, most importantly, 70 months of sobriety.

I quickly joined a home group, attended 90 meetings in 90 days, and spoke at virtually every meeting so people could get to know me. I opened up, accepted help given, and found a sponsor. I found an old-timer who had problems walking and took him a cup of coffee every chance I got. I looked for things to do on a group level and kept in mind my second responsibility, being a dad to three boys.

In this small town, AA is different and yet the same. We have an old-timer who keeps a Big Book in his pocket and makes speeches he never intended. There is no clubhouse, but churches in the area are supportive of AA and offer meeting rooms. In the city, we worked a lot with treatment centers; here, it's the prison system that needs the most attention.

The AA talk is the same here, except they don't say "y'all" as much. Personalities are everywhere but, as I found in the big city, principles lead the way. There is a small coffee shop where I go and usually find AA people talking. Some of the poorest people sit with some of the best-known people in the community and talk the same stuff—getting and staying sober.

One of the best meetings in the area is my home group's Thursday night Grapevine discussion meeting. We read a story from Grapevine and discuss it. It helps me remember that AA works throughout the world.

One son takes karate classes just down the street at the same time I attend a meeting. We get in the car afterward and talk about him: his school, his karate lesson, and his life. I look forward to that meeting after the meeting each week. It's one of the most important ones I attend.

After three years in a small-town community, I have learned that I can stay sober, one day at a time, in the South, the North, the city, or the country. It is not where I got sober that is important, it is how I stay sober today that matters.

*John G.*
*Plattsburgh, New York*

CHAPTER THREE

# Land

Army, Marine and National Guard soldiers getting
and staying sober

---

I n many of Grapevine's military stories, members found their drinking really "took off" once in the service. They write of encountering—to their delight at first—a "permissive" drinking culture, where alcohol is cheap, the legal drinking age is 18 and drinking buddies can always be found. Facing difficult wartime experiences and cut off from family and friends back home, alcohol often became an important friend, who inevitably turned on them. This chapter is a collection of stories by those who served, or are currently serving, in the Army or Marine Corps.

In a story called "New Weapons for a Warrior," Michael T., a young Native American man from Oklahoma, writes about arriving in Vietnam in 1970. For him, "alcohol became my lady, my love and my way to escape problems and fears." He found AA and sobriety after leaving the military. At the time of this story's publication in Grapevine in 1989, Michael writes that he's involved in "the largest Indian veterans' association in the world." Instead of an M-16, his weapons are "love, understanding, compassion, truth and commitment."

In 1991's "One Decent Person," member C.G. of St. Louis, Missouri hits bottom in the Army and is sent to treatment for six weeks. He worries that African-American people like him "never really get sober." But his counselor, an AA member, understands and surprises him with a big hug. At the time he writes his story, he has four years sober.

In the story "Through the Darkest Days," Roger W. had five years of sobriety when the Army sent him to the Middle East. Lonely and isolated, he felt the desire to drink return. Fortunately, he reached out to GSO for help—and was soon inundated with "cards, letters, speaker tapes, literature." He realized that he had a host of friends "who loved me through one of the darkest times in my recovery."

In "I Was a Perpetual Private," member T.C.F. writes that when he enlisted in the Army during the Korean War, he already had "quite a taste for alcohol." A drunken spree lands him in a prison, where two AAs, both soldiers, pay him a visit. In this story from 1966, T.C.F. writes: "I now have nearly four years of sobriety, and I owe it all to the helping hands of AA and the Twelve Steps."

## Through the Darkest Days
May 2005

When I was five years sober, I was 23 years old and I had just been laid off from a seasonal job. I had a new wife and a new child, and had put a college education on hold in order to take care of my family. I was learning to deal with life on life's terms. I was attending meetings regularly, had a home group, and was in service there. My career goals were slipping away and I was struggling to raise a family and pay bills, and hoped to improve the financial situation I was in. Out of desperation, I shared a thought I believed was insanity with my recovering wife. I had told her I was thinking about the military as a solution—that I could have a steady paycheck, get some money for college, and get out in a few years. She thought it was a reasonable idea.

I did not check with anyone in my group or with my sponsor, because I sensed I was being foolish and they would stop me. Nobody in my home group had ever joined the military before. I saw a recruiter from each of the services, and then I went to my home group and I reluctantly shared my recent experiences and what I thought was the solution. We had a podium that seemed to bring the truth out of people when they began sharing.

After the meeting I was told that it was a sane thought, and that I had been sober and active in AA long enough to be able to make such life decisions. My sponsor recommended I take an inventory of the situation and I did. It turned out that the second person I asked to listen to my inventory was the child of a military officer who had grown up in the lifestyle I was considering.

I joined the Army in February 1989 with five years of sobriety. I cried when I said goodbye to my home group. During basic training, I used the chapel as a means of spiritual guidance because meetings were not available. Once I arrived at my first duty station, I followed the directions of those who had been sober and traveled or sober and incarcerated—I found a meeting. I was told that it is critical to find a meeting of Alcoholics Anonymous as soon as possible, and preferably within the first 24 hours of arriving at a new location or leaving an institution. This is important for me because the thought often creeps in that "nobody knows me here."

I called AA before the furniture arrived. I made contact and found there were meetings on base. I have since learned that most military installations have at least one meeting on post and usually several nearby. I had lots of preconceived notions about sober life in the Army, which eventually were replaced with the truth as I gained experience, strength and hope. I did not think it appropriate to go to meetings in uniform, since AA is a place where there are no leaders and there ought to be no rank. Well, when that is the suit you wear all day, it is difficult to change and it is especially impractical to change in the middle of the duty day. I learned that we are all equal inside the rooms anyway. I learned to call people "Mike" in the meeting and "Sir" once we left.

I enjoyed success in the Army, and looking back, I believe it is mostly because I was sober and mature enough to be ready to be a good employee. I had a desire to serve and was put into the personnel administration field.

I had no idea what I wanted to be when I grew up, so I thought the recruiters would give me a test and tell me what I should be. I had rationalized that if they told me I should be a firefighter, it would be God's will and the pressure for me to make a decision would be off. Instead, they told me I tested very well and was qualified for any job they had. They handed me a list of jobs to choose from. All I knew from AA was that I wanted to be of service to God and my fellows. They suggested I be the Chaplain's Assistant. I would have taken it but my misunderstanding of career progression in the military led me to assume that you would someday be promoted to Chaplain, and I didn't think that was for me. Today, our Chaplain's Assistant takes care of the collection, makes coffee after our service, and sets up chairs for our socials. Who knew that these were skills I had already honed back in my original home group?

The office job I had envisioned was not accurate either. I spent over half my first two years in the field with an airborne unit. It was a new and exciting experience to jump out of airplanes. I used the Third Step prayer every single time I jumped and still do to this day. In 1990, we were notified that we were deploying to the Middle East. I was afraid; I had drifted away from AA, and finding my new group did not feel as comfortable as my first home group. I prayed and wrote a letter to the General Service Office asking them to forward a Grapevine and to pray for us. What I got was an incredible experience!

I truly was worried about staying sober, even in a country that was reputed to have no alcohol. Upon arriving, we were very busy, as much of our equipment was still green and had to be painted or exchanged for desert camouflage stuff. We lived in tents at first until a contracting officer could find us a better home. We later moved to an old horse stable, but the cinderblock buildings were a great improvement until the ground war began.

I put a notice on the bulletin board that said, "Friends of Bill W. meet here every night at 1900 hours." I waited with a Big Book in my hand, which I thought was easy to recognize for anyone familiar with AA. Nobody ever came. I relied on my literature and a few tapes through the next few months.

Once, when I was so lonely and desperate, the thought of a drink came into my mind and I began to feel the desire to drink. I considered the choices, considering the black market supply I knew had come from Bahrain, or the near-beer they served in our recreation tent. I began to be consumed by the mental obsession, even after seven years without a drink! I cried myself to sleep that night and postponed the drink for just one more day. "One Day at a Time" truly saved my life, because the next day did not seem so bad. The Scud alerts were becoming more frequent and fear was a real part of my life. Even though these weapons did not turn out to be extremely devastating, the fear at that moment was very real. I took the Big Book and a picture of my family to the bunker every time there was an alarm.

About this time, the miracle began to occur, just when I needed it the most. I began to receive my first pieces of mail from members of AA who got my address from the Loners-Internationalist program at GSO. This is what our General Service Office did for me when I wrote and asked for help. They placed my name and address along with other service members on a list and circulated it among trusted servants in the Fellowship. The result was that when I put off that drink for one more day, I began to get the love of our Fellowship delivered in a mail pouch. At first it was a few letters and a card from an AA group. This was enough to give me hope. As the days went on the amount of mail increased. I was now getting cards, letters, speaker tapes, literature, and even a care package with goodies in it. I often got five to 10 pieces of mail in a day, although the delivery was sporadic and we usually only received mail three times a week. At the peak of this postal miracle, I got 36 pieces of mail from AA members all over the country. My fellow soldiers did not know why I was getting so much mail. I told them I had a fan club. Actually I did; I had a host of friends who loved me through one of the darkest times in my recovery, even though they had never laid eyes on me in their lives. We still shared a common bond and they were able to send the hand of AA halfway around the world to be there.

I returned home safe and sound as most of us did during that war. I continued on in my military career and still serve after 16 years. So much for getting the college money and moving on.

I have found that the military is a great place to serve Alcoholics Anonymous. I am successful in my profession and have been blessed to pass my experience, strength and hope on to many uniformed and civilian alcoholics. During each deployment I have been familiar with since my own experience, I seek to repay those who helped me by sending letters and literature and seeking out those who might be trying to not drink a day at a time.

Today there are many military members serving in harm's way who have battled with alcoholism and been defeated. Alcoholics Anonymous has worked to help us meet calamity with serenity in a variety of circumstances. Since World War II, members of AA have used literature to help carry the massage of hope to our servicemen and women in recovery. From my own experiences and many observations, they will return transformed in some way.

*Roger W.*
*Shape, Belgium*

## I Better Get a Kiss Out of This
April 2014

I never thought I had a drinking problem. Everybody drank a lot in the Army. On a Friday night at the officers' club, everybody drank more than they should have, and by the end of the evening I was usually still ready to keep going. I never really thought I drank differently from most people. I was always at work on time, and even though it took a couple cups of coffee to get me going, by noon I was always feeling OK.

However, I did notice that even when I had no intention of having more than a glass or two of wine at dinner, I would end up having a bottle or two. That bothered me a little, but at my favorite piano bar in Carmel, California, it was not unusual to see many others do the same thing.

I had a friend there named Bob. I worried about him because he used to keep a jug of wine in his car and would take slugs from it every couple of minutes or so. He seemed to have a perpetual buzz on, and I never saw him when he wasn't drinking, so I thought he might be an alcoholic. I definitely didn't drink like Bob. That much I knew.

One day my artillery commander said to me, "You look mighty tired today lieutenant colonel. Are you feeling OK? Did you stay out a little late last night?" "No sir," I replied. "Maybe I have a little touch of the flu."

Hmmm, I thought, that's not good; my boss noticed I was not doing so well. So I tried to drink just on weekends for a while, but I couldn't do it. The idea of not drinking at all didn't seem like an option to me. I told myself I had a lot on my mind: my divorce, the nightmares about Vietnam, and the bills that seemed to never go away. I worked hard, and at the end of the day I had earned that glass of wine. I also had a lot of fun when I was drinking. I was wittier, a better dancer, and a lot less shy. I wasn't sure I could be the life of the party unless I drank, especially with the fun-loving crowd I hung around with at my piano bar. What the heck, I wasn't carrying a jug of wine around in my car like Bob.

One weekend when I came into the bar, one of my buddies said, "Hey George, you were a riot last night when you got up on the table and sang." "Uh, yeah" I replied, "a riot." I tried to remember the incident, but I just couldn't. I also couldn't remember driving home. That scared me. For the first time it occurred to me that I might really have a problem, but I quickly put it out of my mind. I couldn't imagine my life without drinks to have a good time.

The truth was that I wasn't having as good a time as I used to. Drinking was becoming an end in itself. It especially wasn't fun looking for my frigging car when I had no idea where I'd parked it. It was getting harder to get to work every morning. And my boss was beginning to give me strange looks. I tried to cut back. One week, I didn't have a drink until Friday came. Then I felt I deserved a reward. A couple of glasses of wine at dinner really felt great and before I knew it, I had two empty bottles at my table. I sang a few songs at the bar, decided to go home, and woke up in jail.

What the hell was I doing on the floor in a jail cell? I couldn't remember a thing. The next morning, they told me I had been driving erratically, had been pulled over, failed a field sobriety test (turns out the alphabet has 26 letters, not 12), and I would be going to court soon.

All the drunk-driving violations of military personnel—especially officers—ended up on the General's desk. Before I knew it I was reporting to him and he was telling me, "Lieutenant colonel, you've disgraced your uniform. If this ever happens again, I'll make sure you lose your commission and your retirement."

I was completely ashamed. I promised the General and myself that I would never drink and drive again. That Friday at the piano bar I told myself that I would have just one, two at the most. Several hours later, I was driving home drunk. Holy crap, I thought, if I get caught I will throw away almost 20 years in the service. Luckily I made it home, but as I lay in my bed I realized my drinking had gotten out of control. My life was unmanageable. I was scared to death, but still I was not giving up my wine.

The next weekend I went home to visit my mom. I liked that, because whenever I went there she would fix me up with one of her friends' cute daughters. This time was no exception. When I picked up my date to go to dinner she asked me if I would mind going to a short meeting with her that she really needed to attend before dinner. What the heck, no problem I told her. She was very cute.

"What kind of meeting?" I asked.

"An AA meeting," she said.

"You mean ... like Alcoholics Anonymous?"

"Yes, it's only an hour," she said. "And then we can hit the town."

For years my mom had been telling me I had a drinking problem, and now look what she did! Anyway, I thought, what can it hurt? She's darn cute.

The next thing I knew I was in a room with the Twelve Steps hanging on a wall and the slogan "Let go and let God." Man, I thought, I better at least get a goodnight kiss out of this.

The funny thing was, the people in the room didn't look like alcoholics. They were well-dressed, well-spoken and seemed pretty damn happy. So I listened to what they were saying. Since they introduced me as a newcomer, Step One became the topic of the meeting. When the chair of the meeting read, "We admitted we were powerless over alcohol and that our lives had become unmanageable," that got my attention. My life was unmanageable. I listened to them tell their stories. Some sounded much worse than me and some sounded just like me. I felt like I was on a different planet, but I had a crazy feeling that maybe I was finally really home. When my turn came going around the table, I surprised myself when I said, "My name is George, and I'm an alcoholic."

The strangest sensation came over me. I didn't believe in religion then, and I still don't. But something happened to me that day. The desire to drink left me, as if by magic, and I felt a new fellowship with my fellow human beings. I didn't know at the moment that I had found a new way to operate my life.

Now, many years later, I realize it was the beginning of my new life. After the meeting, my date and I went to dinner. As we were sitting in the restaurant, I looked around at the other diners with their cocktails and beer and asked her, "I can never, really never, ever have a drink again?" She smiled sweetly and said, "No silly, not forever. It's just for today, one day at a time."

We both laughed. And, oh yeah, I did get a very nice kiss goodnight!

*George K.*
*Magnolia, Texas*

## Merry Christmas
*(From: Dear Grapevine)*
December 1962

On the first of January I will be 50 years of age and thus retired from the Armed Forces because of age. Day by day, with the help of my Higher Power, I pray that I will be sober for this occasion.

I would like to thank AA and its founders, my sponsor, who happens to be my sister, and all the members of AA in the Armed Forces for having helped me to stay sober from 1956 to 1962 so I am now able to retire with an honorable discharge and draw my pension.

Because I was always on the go and at times could not be attached to a group I relied on Grapevine to bring me the message, which constantly reminded me that somewhere throughout the world some other servicemen were trying hard, with the help of AA, to keep sober and thus pursue their service career.

I know hundreds of servicemen who are AA members and who have had sobriety for years yet do not own the Big Book and have no Grapevine to read every month. I say that without these two weapons I could not guarantee how long I could have stayed sober. At this time of the year I would like to wish all servicemen and the staffs of the New York offices a very Merry Christmas and a Happy New 1963.

If ever you should come to this city do drop in to say hello and see how I am faring now in civilian life.

*G. N.*
*Montreal, Quebec*

## The Password Was "AA"

October 1957

In a military hospital for the second time for alcoholism, I became intimate with AA.

Another serviceman and myself were in the "icebox" together, going through a cooling-off period. We were both at the end of our ropes. We both knew what we had to do to save ourselves from an adverse Service discharge, eventual insanity or an unavoidable slow death if we kept on drinking. We finally came to the conclusion that we couldn't go on that way.

When we were able to accept coffee, we found a place to sit down and drink it. We had many discussions about AA, our adventures with booze, and the terrible physical and mental suffering following a bender. The two of us decided that the only place left for us to go was a smoke-filled coffee room full of alcoholics. Something bigger than both of us must have been hanging over our heads because, during one of our talks over coffee in the ward kitchen where we were recuperating, one of the attendants on duty overheard a mention of AA. His ears perked up like a hunting dog's. He came over to us and related the fact that his mother had been in AA for two years. He suggested that if we would like someone to visit us from her group he would see her about it. We were only too happy to hear this and we gave him the go-ahead sign.

The following days were pretty well-packed with action for us. We must have had at least four or five pairs of visitors each day for seven days.

A government reservation is pretty prohibitive when it comes to allowing civilians free run of its grounds. The ward we were in was a locked ward since the inmates were mostly mental cases. In order for a civilian to gain access to this ward, a pass signed by the Commanding Officer and countersigned. by the Security Officer must be presented. Even then the mufti-wearing individual is watched like a hawk. Visitors are obliged to observe visiting hours and comply with many regulations. Not so with our AA friends!

These wonderful people came at all hours, through all entrances, on any day. They came at 10 o'clock in the morning, 11 o'clock at night or any hour inbetween. They passed through the main gate without a pass, without mentioning anyone's name attached to the hospital and without influence. They gained entrance to the locked ward, sans pass, and were in general moving around that hospital as though it belonged to them. It was amazing! This was something we had never seen before. The men in uniform didn't get around the way these magicians did. We asked each other how in heck they did it. We found out later that AAs are not civilians in the true sense of the word. We also discovered that a very simple verbal formula was used by them in getting through the gate and into the locked ward. It was a sentence ending with the first letter of the alphabet repeated twice: "We came to see someone. We are from AA."

Our friends used these open sesame words until we were able to get out to meetings on our own. Neither my pal nor myself will ever forget the hope and comfort these people gave to us in those first few horrible days in the hospital. These swell people, by giving their time and part of themselves and through the use of magic words, brought hope and temporary peace of mind to the two of us. In doing this they enabled us both to step out of the hospital with our best foot forward.

*E. J. C.*
*New York, New York*

## The Colonel Was a Lush

February 1961

I am on a two-week tour of duty at the Pentagon. I am a Lieutenant Colonel now, and this is my second promotion since I was released from wartime duty and reverted to reserve status. I have been granted a security clearance of the highest order, after being subjected to the required background investigation.

All this is a source of pride and satisfaction to me, because I am an alcoholic. My long stay overseas seems to have been related to the accelerated progress of my disease. Liquor was plentiful and cheap, and the permissive atmosphere enabled me to get away with excesses otherwise not to be condoned. Like a naughty child, I reveled in being bad—and getting away with it. But stories of wartime escapades (such as waking up clad only in my underwear, at five in the morning, to find myself locked into the officers' club in a strange city) were followed by postwar misery (for who could delight in telling of a Christmas Day spent in the nut ward of a service hospital?)

Disgrace followed degradation, and I was sent home. Now I have a source of reassurance and satisfaction in redeeming my sorry performance by a life that has given me indications of public trust, and some degree of professional reputation in my military specialty.

Redemption of the sorry past by the present good was made mine as a gift through Alcoholics Anonymous. The Higher Power is forgiving when we accept his guidance—for do we not pray, "Thy will be done"?

I want to tell other servicemen, past and present, about my coming into AA, and the good it has brought me, because I know there are many members of the armed forces, whether active, reserve, or retired, who feel as I did, that they have besmirched their military careers and reputations through alcoholic drinking.

Some of us did active harm to ourselves and others because drink affected our effectiveness in combat. Others suffered in a quieter, more protracted way because alcohol gradually sapped their strength and spirit. On some an official mark of censure was laid; others escaped active blame, but had their progress slowed or stopped.

I had no demerits, bad efficiency reports, or discharge papers to be kept secret. I had a record of hospitalization for attempted suicide (inability to adjust to postwar conditions, they called it) and a later appeal to the Veterans Administration for treatment of my shaky nerves. I felt sick at heart when I saw this spelled out in impersonal detail in my 201 file.

The veteran, no matter what the effect of his alcoholic drinking, regrets the blurring of his reputation and loss of privilege. If he is also interested in gaining sobriety, he probably wants to do something about clarifying his situation.

For me, I wanted sobriety above all. Lord, was I sick of my tired, dirty, smelly, hopeless self! With my membership in AA came a great interest in its workings. It was good to find references to AA in service publications, and I was delighted to read the Twelve Steps in a joint Army-Air Force manual. The growing roster of AA groups at service installations and communities here and overseas impresses me. I have visited some of these, and benefited greatly from the contact with AAs in uniform.

There is a bond within a bond when servicemen meet in AA. The shared background of military life combines with our memories of the common problem to tie us together. It's even fun to laugh now at some of the horrible scrapes I got myself into. (For a while they'd put me back on the bar stool, but later they tired of picking me up off the floor and would throw me in the back of the jeep. One night the CO found me there in the rain, out colder than the rain itself).

To my fellow servicemen, I want to say that I felt a great relief when I dragged the skeleton out of the closet. To be sure, seeing my 201 file was a shock, but it led me to talk with a medical officer. I was ashamed, and wanted to know how my past record would affect my staying in the reserves. He told me that my record of misbehavior was being balanced, and slowly overcome, by the record I was building up for reliability and enthusiasm.

I had neither quality when I was drinking. Did you?

The medical officer's comments, and other indications that things could get better, encouraged me to continue to place my faith in AA and to keep on rebuilding my personal and business life, as well as my reserve activities. All the time, AA and its meetings were there to give me help.

It makes me happy to find that my family, my business associates, my friends, and my country look upon me now with favor.

They're not looking at me with approval—they're looking at a grateful member of Alcoholics Anonymous, brought back to life through its blessed workings.

But that's my secret—I didn't tell this to the people in the Pentagon!

*J. S.*
*Bedford Hills, New York*

## One Decent Person

*(From: Dear Grapevine)*
December 1991

I am a single black man, 26 years old. I hit bottom in the armed services, where I was sent to treatment for six weeks as an in-patient. During the first week or so I became worried that other black people never really get sober. As if it were new to me, I realized after six months of not drinking that I was a black man. I went to my counselor who was also an AA member, but he already understood my problem before I did.

I'm 6'2", about 200 pounds, and he was too. When he saw me in the hall he would hug me firmly. I could not believe he would do that. Officers didn't do that, men didn't do that, people of a different race didn't do that. So there I was faced with myself. I said if there is one decent person in the world there may be others. He broke down a wall of isolation that I pray shall never return. I am sober four years now.

*C. G.*
*St. Louis, Missouri*

## New Weapons for a Warrior
March 1989

When I was a young boy growing up in Oklahoma City, Oklahoma, I felt as if I were different. That feeling was intensified by being poor and being an American Indian. I was raised in a nonalcoholic household, but the only thing that was missing was the alcohol. There were cursing, accusations, and big fights all the time. I could hardly wait until I was old enough to be on my own. My father, whom I now love dearly, tried his best with what he had. My mother, whom I also love dearly, just tried to survive.

I married at the age of 20 because my girlfriend was pregnant, but also because I loved her. Things didn't work out because my drinking intensified and I became abusive. Needless to say, she didn't put up with that for very long, and I was soon separated from her. With no way to pay child support, I was looking at a jail sentence. Our two lawyers put their heads together and figured that the best thing for all parties concerned was for me to go into the service so my ex-wife and child could receive economic support from the U.S. Army.

After basic training and A.I.T., I was lean, mean, and part of the "Green Machine." I was ready to go to war and defend this great nation of ours. In October 1970, I left Fort Lewis, Washington for Vietnam. Again, alcohol became my lady, my love, and my way to escape problems and fears. After all, I was in a place where people were shooting at me, with real bullets. I became a hardened vet and thought I had met my calling. I was a real warrior and I even had the medals to prove it. Little did I realize that the chemical addiction was sizing me up for the kill. I became the hunted, instead of the hunter.

I completed my tour and rotated back to the States. As soon as I stepped off of the plane in San Francisco, a woman came up to me, spat on my medals, and cried, "Baby killer." Needless to say, I became very bitter about society, the Army, and the way I felt this country had treated the Vietnam veterans after they came home. Again I was judged by a society that I had no control over. First it was the color of my skin, then because vets were classified as mindless killers and junkies. I felt this was the last indignity. The only people who gave me a welcome home were my Indian people, because veterans in my culture are held in high regard.

But my drinking became more frequent, along with the flashbacks and nightmares about Vietnam. My fits of anger and despair became worse and I started to fear for my sanity. On three separate occasions, I held a weapon to my head and wanted to end it all. I was virtually at the end of my rope and slipping fast. I knew how to kill the enemy. Could I now kill the worst enemy of all—myself? For some reason, I never could get the courage to do it, and I continued to drink.

In 1979, I was exposed to Alcoholics Anonymous through the Cheyenne-Arapaho Treatment Center. I was in and out of the program until 1983 when I was hospitalized in Clinton, Oklahoma. I was literally bleeding to death. For once, when someone said something to me, it jibed. The doctor came into my room after he examined me from the inside with a camera and said, "Mike, I don't care what you do, but if you don't stop drinking, you'll be dead in six to 12 months." That gave me an awareness I had never experienced before. I was also aware that because I had wanted to be so in control of my own life, I had become totally out of control. That was August 10, 1983 and I had had my last drink two days earlier.

Through the Fellowship of AA, I have not had an excuse to take a drink since that date. I now have four sponsors, something I never had before. Ironically, the place where I was first exposed to treatment and AA is where I work now as a drug and alcoholism counselor. Through this program, I have gotten back in touch with my Higher Power and have been able to take part in spiritual ceremonies with my Arapaho people. I have completed my Sundance Vow for myself and have been made a ceremonial grandfather for other sundancers. I also take part in ceremonial "sweat lodges." I am an officer in the largest Indian veterans' association in the world and work with a lot of alcoholic Vietnam veterans. I incorporate native healing methods, as well as Alcoholics Anonymous, as part of the therapy.

I am 39 years old and still becoming a warrior. Not through perfection, but through progress. When I was in Vietnam, I wore a T-shirt that read: "Yea, though I walk through the valley of the shadow of death, I will fear no evil, for I am the roughest, toughest, meanest SOB in that valley." Today, my strength comes from surrendering. The war I'm fighting today is with drug addiction and alcoholism. It's the toughest battle I've ever fought because this enemy is not seen or heard. I can't fight this disease with my fists or with conventional weapons. The only way I can win this war is to admit unconditional defeat. Instead of carrying an M-16 automatic ride, my weapons today are love, understanding, compassion, truth and commitment.

I'm happy to say that there are more and more of my Indian people who are joining the ranks of Alcoholics Anonymous. My Indian people were once a strong, proud and dignified nation, but alcohol was beating many of us. Now my people are once again becoming a proud nation. In admitting our defects, we are winning.

In Vietnam and on the battlefield, I was a good soldier. It's different now. I am finally becoming a warrior.

*Michael T.*
*Concho, Oklahoma*


# I Was a Perpetual Private
May 1966

I enlisted in the Army at an early age, while the Korean conflict was in high gear. Through high school I developed quite a taste for alcohol, and in the Army I devoted most of my off-duty and some of my on-duty time to the consumption of it. Needless to say, this resulted in some foggy days, a number of reductions in rank, and a few severe chewings out.

I married at the age of 22 and managed for a year or so to hide my heavy drinking from my wife. Of course, it all came to a head, and after five years of marriage, four children, numerous broken promises, heartaches and nearly a nervous breakdown, my wife decided she'd had enough. And I agreed, but I didn't know what to do, or where my true problem lay. She took the children home to mama, and stayed. I tripped merrily off to a new assignment in the South. I had eight and a half years of service and had achieved the rank of private E2.

A rapid promotion to private first class at my new station convinced me that all was OK again, and that I was just about the best damn soldier in the Army at that time, and that I was well on my way back up. I celebrated too heavily one night and borrowed an automobile and forgot to return it, forgetting at the same time to report for duty for about 10 straight days. I was apprehended of course, and the auto theft resulted in a 60-day stint on a road gang in our fine southern prison system, plus the prospect of a dishonorable discharge from the Army when I returned to duty.

I found, though, that in this prison they had Alcoholics Anonymous meetings, and also, what at the time appeared much more to my liking, after the meeting they gave out coffee and doughnuts. I allowed myself to be persuaded to go to the meeting for the latter. And here is where fate stepped in! It just so happened that the two speakers that night were military, and I was caught spellbound in the almost complete reenactment of my life. Here were two people who had done the same things and suffered the same as I had, yet they had found the solution to their problem. I was impressed, and continued to attend meetings, not for the refreshments, but for the meat of the subject.

I was released to military authorities and returned to my former unit, and here again, fate intervened. My C.O. had heard of AA and how it worked, and instead of processing me out of the service, he gave me that "one more chance," and I grabbed it like a man going down for the third time.

I now have nearly four years of sobriety, and I owe it all to the helping hands of AA and the Twelve Steps, some of which at times seem impossible to work, but eventually I find I can attempt them.

My wife and I are happily reunited, and we now have five children, a dog and a new home. I have a respected position in the Army, with the rank to go along with it. And last, but surely not least, I have the self-respect that I so sorely sought in those old jumbled days.

Sometimes it gets a little tough to stay sober, and I have to reach back and pluck out the wise things my sponsors taught me. It's a little tough now, for I'm in Vietnam, but my answers still come through from loners and AAs all over the world, for this is what fellowship means—to share with others.

I'm sober now, and God willing, I'll be sober till the day I die— thanks to AA.

*T. C. F.*
*Vietnam*

## Tough Enough
October 2017

When I first started thinking seriously of joining the Marine Corps, I had three years of sobriety under my belt. The people closest to me in AA suggested the Corps might not be the best option because it is where a lot of people learn to drink, especially in the infantry. My AA friends were concerned the move would affect my sobriety.

I always heard in meetings not to make any big changes in my first few years of sobriety. But that never made sense to me. Our Big Book even had us do the opposite. First, we had to give up drinking and that was a huge change. Then, we had to turn our will and our lives over to a God of our own understanding. That alone was asking a lot for a guy who didn't grow up believing in God. After that, I had to tell another man some of my deepest darkest secrets that I had planned to take to the grave. Later on, I had to face my wrongs and make them right. And several of my wrongs potentially involved me being locked up for a long time.

These were all huge changes that were necessary for me to stay sober. But I had a new relationship with my creator. I felt that I had the tools needed to remain sober while fighting for our country. So I joined the Corps.

Being well-grounded from my home group, I got on the bus to go to boot camp and was feeling in fit spiritual condition. However, the moment I stepped off the bus and on the yellow footsteps, all that conditioning slipped away.

Boot camp felt like being a prisoner of war, with everything you love being just outside the gate. I was introduced to a new level of fear. The purpose of boot camp is to break down the civilian person so they can build you back up as a Marine. Needless to say, the drill instructors were very good at what they did. They worked us relentlessly. I lost over 30 pounds in 13 weeks.

The only thing that kept me going was that at night I had a routine of reviewing my day and keeping a close contact with my Higher Power. As an alcoholic, I don't know if I would have kept my sanity without that.

After surviving boot camp, I went back to my home group and had a tough time holding down my ego. I was very proud, doing everything from wearing Marine Corps shirts to making sure I mentioned my experiences in all my shares and all my conversations. Every time I mentioned being a Marine, people felt obligated to give their thanks and support.

Although I was sitting at four years of sobriety at that point, I let the Marine Corps distract me from our singleness of purpose, which is to help the alcoholic still suffering. Over the next couple of years, I only went to a handful of meetings and that was just to show my face and leave. My priorities quickly shifted to chasing women, competitive fighting and being the "tough guy" I thought I had to be. I didn't realize this at the time, but I became the alcoholic who still suffered.

I was entering my last year on my contract and received deployment orders to get shipped to the Middle East. Normally, this is something every Marine was excited about. However, I was put into a position of leadership and once again I was full of fear.

I had enough AA in me to know that I couldn't lead anyone if my head wasn't in the right place. So I contacted our chaplain and the Substance Abuse Control Officer to find out if there were any AA meetings organized as one of the services. To my surprise there wasn't anything at all. And so I worked with them to create a new meeting called "Friends of Bill."

I had no idea how this was going to work, especially with keeping anonymity when the only people who could attend were the people I was currently deployed with. The chaplain sponsored the meeting so that we could legally have it in confidence. That helped a lot. It ensured that we couldn't get in trouble for anything that was said during the meeting.

I contacted GSO and AA members back home for literature, speaker tapes and Grapevine magazines. After everything was set, it hit me that I might be the only person on this deployment who had any experience with staying sober in AA. And I felt like I barely knew anything about it.

Looking back, I can see that this new meeting was one of the most pivotal moments in my sobriety because it sparked in me an overwhelming desire to get into the rest of the literature that I'd been ignoring for years. It's kind of like getting your first sponsee, the feeling that you can't float by anymore and you need to walk the walk.

I studied everything from pamphlets to the many AA books. I learned there is way more to this program than just reading the Big Book and going to meetings. I started falling in love with the Traditions and the Concepts of service. I started connecting the dots to see the bigger AA picture.

It was a little strange at first because I had to make sure that all who attended knew and felt they were equal. We were just a group of alcoholics trying to recover. There was no rank or seniority. We went by first names and identified as alcoholics. To build trust and to demonstrate that this meeting was a safe place, I opened some of the shares with some information that would have gotten me in trouble if word spread outside the meeting. And at the end of the meeting, I had to make it clear that rank and the uniformed code of military justice had to be respected and applied.

It was a hard transition sometimes because in the meeting I was open, loving and tolerant, while earlier in the day I had been yelling at half of them for not moving fast enough, which was expected of me as part of my job. At first, most people who attended were sent by their command because they had a drinking-related charge against them. Many of these people weren't really interested in AA. But as we went through the Big Book, listened to everyone's stories and started identifying some of the problems and suggesting solutions, several of the guys asked if we could meet three times a week instead of just once.

Some days were tough. We lost some close friends and were put into situations that seemed to be on the other end of living a spiritual life. Our faith was tried and tested. But because we had each other, in the end our faith was polished into something that can never be taken away.

I am beyond grateful for all the men and women who came before me, those who went through the trial and error of finding out what works and what doesn't. On top of that, they took the time to write their experiences down so that when I needed a program of recovery I had a place to go to. And because of that, five of the guys who had never attended a meeting of AA before deployment are now celebrating two years of sobriety this month.

My experience of service in AA has me hooked. When I came home, I immediately jumped into general service. A group of us are now on a committee to bring AA to other military members. One of my favorite discoveries I found when I got into the literature was the Responsibility Declaration on the back of pamphlets: It says, "When anyone, anywhere, reaches out for help, I want the hand of AA always to be there."

*Coty Q.*
*Irvine, California*

## We Were All Just Drunks
May 2005

"Eyes front, focused into infinity!" Our drill sergeant shouted at us, a long line of privates standing in line for morning chow. We stood at parade rest, our hands locked behind us in the small of our backs. Despite the name, it was really no way to rest, and rest was the one thing on all of our minds. I was 19 years old in Army basic training at Fort Bliss, another Army misnomer.

When I joined the Army National Guard in 1989, I was already several years sober, having joined AA at the age of 15. In the months leading up to boot camp, my mouth filled with canker sores, a symptom of the stress I was feeling, I'd read in the Big Book that sober AAs had weathered the trials of military life without a drink, but I couldn't imagine that I would be able to go so long without a meeting and not become a dry drunk. I was also worried that nobody else would understand my situation. I pictured myself explaining HALT to a maniacal drill sergeant and shivered.

In the first few weeks of boot camp, I discovered that the morning chow line was the only place I'd get a little bit of quiet. The drill sergeants were too tired to bust our chops much, and we weren't allowed to speak. We were supposed to study little training manuals that we carried in our cargo pockets, but most people stared at the pages and fantasized about sleeping. It was in those minutes of calm that I read my pocket version of the "Twelve and Twelve." I said the Steps to myself and then the Traditions. I'd read a few paragraphs and picture myself back home in a meeting and imagine what I might say about what I'd just read. It was a little meeting in my head and it did me a world of good.

My first real test was our weekend pass at the end of boot camp. Without even trying, I had gravitated toward the drunks and found myself in a dark bar in El Paso. When the pitchers of beer arrived, my friends stared grim-faced at the beer and began their task. There wasn't any talking; they just poured their beers and started in. I stepped outside and found a pay phone. I called information and got the number for Alcoholics Anonymous. It wasn't that I wanted to drink, but I knew that things would only get more boring in the bar, and since I had no plans of getting a haircut, I didn't want to spend any more time in the barbershop than I had to.

A fellow AA picked me up and took me to a meeting. It felt great to be in a meeting after nearly three months without one. I was so exhausted that I kept nodding off during the meeting, but nobody seemed to mind. I soon discovered that all around me sat officers, the men I'd been trained to respect to the point of fear in basic training. Full bird colonels and majors shared about their drinking; they shook my hand and welcomed me. In that meeting, we were all just drunks. It shocked me at first, but as I heard everyone's story I was reminded once again that alcoholism is an equal opportunity employer. It doesn't care a thing about your pay-grade, and so nobody pulls rank in AA.

I stayed sober throughout my training and returned to my home state stronger then ever. My heart goes out to the troops in Iraq right now. I pray for them all, but I also know that no matter what happens, they don't have to drink. AA will be waiting for them, just like it waited for me when I went away to train.

*Sean B.*
*Kalamazoo, Michigan*

## MAASH

October 2017

As a reserve Army Medical Officer, I attended two weeks annual training, known as AT, each summer. One hot July, AT was in Massachusetts at Fort Devens. I was Chief Medical Officer for my MASH unit. Our job at AT was to erect and operate a portable tent hospital. I always brought three books with me: my

Big Book, the *Twelve Steps and Twelve Traditions* and *Twenty-Four Hours A Day.*

Our company had almost 450 reservists. At the first morning formation, I announced the time for sick call. The new unit chaplain followed and introduced himself. "I'm your new Army chaplain," he said. "Ladies and gentlemen of the 116th MASH facility, we must all remember that we are people as well as soldiers with a medical mission. We bring to AT human anxieties, worries and earthly concerns only God can help with. Each evening at 1900 hours, I will hold a session in the chapel tent for anyone who wants to air perceived problems for us, as a group, to offer solutions."

Unusual noises resounded from the "at attention" MASH company. There were coughs, cleared throats, burps and intestinal sounds, which, all put together, sounded like musical toilets flushing at the same time. The chaplain repeated his invitation and dismissed the company.

"Chaplain, have you done this before?" I asked. It was new to me and I had been in the military reserve for 15 years.

"This is my first AT in the Army Reserve, doctor, I mean Colonel. I want to treat the soldiers as humans and remind them that the soldiers they treat are also people. If they resolve any stressful problems they brought with them, they can objectively do their job better."

"And where did you learn this, Chaplain?" I asked.

"I'm working on my master's thesis on the premise that people are God's children wherever they go, and whatever workforce capacity they find themselves in," he replied.

"Well, good luck." I told him. "I have to go now. Oh, it's OK to just call me 'Doc' instead of Colonel. It helps me maintain the proper rapport with my groups. They're all doctors, physician assistants, nurses, nurses' aides, all intermixed with everything from stretcher-bearers to pharmacists."

The chaplain saluted and went to the chapel tent. That evening, 1900 hours had come and gone. Out of curiosity, I went to the chapel tent. The chaplain was almost asleep in a chair behind his desk.

"Any luck, Chaplain? It's 2130 hours."

He turned his tired young face toward me. "No Doc, no one showed up. I can't understand why not even one person responded," he said. "Everyone has problems." The next night was also fruitless for the chaplain.

Several reservists I knew from AA had asked me to hold an AA meeting, but I had no place to conduct it there at Fort Devens. I immediately thought of the chaplain.

Seeing the chaplain very sullen, I said, "Chaplain, I think I can get people into your tent tonight. I know many reservists who would like a place to air the stress in their lives."

"You have my permission," he said, then gave me a pleading look. "Can I come, sir?"

"Of course," I replied. "It'll be an open meeting."

We had to send for extra chairs. Not only were there AA members from my home group there, but an equally large number of reservists arrived who were from different home towns.

A surgical nurse asked to chair the meeting. "I'd like to welcome all AA members and members of the 116th MASH Hospital Company to our first Fort Devens AA field meeting," she said. "I'd also like to thank the chaplain for the meeting place."

I looked over to the chaplain. He was mouthing the letters "AA" with a puzzled look on his face.

The meeting chair continued through the opening Serenity Prayer, Preamble, "How It Works" and the Twelve Traditions. She then asked the group for a topic for discussion. Several hands were raised. Anger, resentment and frustration were voiced as topics. The meeting chair settled on "identifying and processing feelings without alcohol."

This gave way to a discussion of a variety of good feelings like gratitude and hope, intermixed with negative entities like anger. The majority of those sharing voiced how AA helps us live without alcohol and use a Higher Power, a God of our understanding, to bring us together in an Army camp, where a nightly choice of revelry and drinking in town were active alternatives.

"I can't believe it," the chaplain said, as he gazed at the large number of reservists who had shared their experience, strength and hope through AA. At the end of the meeting, the chaplain was again thanked for the use of his tent. He was overwhelmed.

"Doc, I had no idea AA was like this," he said and swatted a mosquito. "We were taught to direct alcoholics to AA, but not necessarily to attend. I thought they just talked about drinking. Tonight I heard many people discuss how life improved without using alcohol, and how they used spirituality and each other to cope with life one day at a time."

At the next morning's formation, the chaplain announced, "A nightly AA meeting will take place in the chapel tent. I have also put in a requisition for a bigger tent."

I couldn't resist asking him more about his feelings toward AA. "Well, Chaplain, are you going to mention AA in your master's thesis?"

"Absolutely, Doc," he replied. "Can I reference those three AA books you guys talk about at your meetings?"

"As long as the words cited from them are accurate and referenced appropriately," I answered.

He rubbed his chin. "You know Doc, for a moment last night, I wished I was a recovering alcoholic, so I could have a place like that to go to every night," he said, then touched his crucifix. "People avoid the chaplain at AT. But after last night's AA meeting, there must have been 50 who greeted me at breakfast this morning. Those Twelve Steps should be for all people, not just alcoholics."

I looked at him and said, "Chaplain, we say the same thing in AA."

We both smiled. The chaplain did have to get a larger tent, especially when word went out that an open AA meeting applied to anyone who had a desire to stop drinking.

*Peter G.*
*San Antonio, Texas*

CHAPTER FOUR

# Sea

AA members who serve their country in
the Navy or Coast Guard

---

**W**hether on the water far from land or beneath the sea, these members often got and stayed sober without ready access (or any access at all) to the Fellowship or meetings. They were frequently on their own. They reached for our literature, worked on their relationship with a Higher Power and searched out other alcoholics to help. Their efforts give special meaning to the much-loved phrase in our Big Book: "What we really have is a daily reprieve contingent on the maintenance of our spiritual condition." The stories in this chapter are from members who served in the military at sea.

In the story "AA Under Water," member Bill O. of Key West, Florida takes us along to the regular meeting of the Dolphin Group, which meets twice weekly in a submarine while on training exercises at sea. He and his shipmates spend long weeks at sea in a submarine where "restlessness grows" and "nerves are on edge." Yet Bill finds these meetings down below help "renew their emotional stability." And, he writes, a Higher Power "is present, even beneath the sea."

Rick S. of Groton, Connecticut writes in "How Deep Does Your Sobriety Go?" how the Navy assigned him with a year of sobriety to a submarine. At sea, he learned that his wife back home had given birth to their son—and that both were in "guarded condition." He says his alcoholism came back "with all the fury of a hurricane." With no other AA to talk to, he says he had to find a new level of contact with a power greater than himself. News eventually arrived that his wife and son were all right.

*In the story "And Then We Were Five," Art C. of Nova Scotia, a sailor in the Canadian Navy, writes that he was the only AA member on his ship for two years, serving a tour of duty in Europe. Art would contact AA members when he got to port to "keep my sanity." Then one day, Art was asked to visit a fellow shipmate in sickbay. It turned out to be his first Twelfth Step at sea. By the end of the week, three more sailors asked him for help. When their ship reached port in Gillingham, England, Art brought his four fellow sailors with him to a local AA meeting.*

## AA Under Water
December 1958

A U.S. Navy submarine, diesels pounding, glides swiftly toward its rendezvous. There are no hitches, for the crew know their jobs well. The sub twists and turns, seeking shelter in the depths—spiraling first this way, then that. There are no explosions to smash lights and valves, for this is peacetime ... merely another training routine.

The engine rooms are silent now and the men reminisce over the last liberty port, make plans for the next. Others swap sea stories over coffee. In the radio room a ritual is being performed—strange for submarine life. The radioman pulls out a heavy wooden mallet from under a locker. He sets this on a narrow shelf. Next he lifts out a thick blue book and sets it alongside the mallet. Finally he posts a small sign on the door.

All is ready now and in a little while two crew members enter, each carrying a cup of coffee. One squats on the deck, for the cramped space doesn't allow more than two chairs. No greetings are necessary, for these men live side by side in a hollow pipe some 300 feet long, day and night. One man bangs the mallet, says a few words and all three bow their heads for a moment of silent prayer.

The sign on the door reads: "AA Meeting Tonight." The mallet is the Chairman's gavel, and the blue book is a copy of *Alcoholics Anonymous*. This is the "Dolphin" group of AA, named after the emblem of the Submarine Service, meeting as all AA groups do to "solve their common problem and help others to recover from alcoholism."

The members are the same as you would find in any AA group. One had been pronounced "hopeless" several years before by Navy doctors. He has been sober 19 months. The second was on the verge of his first trip to the psycho ward. He has been sober four months. The third was well along the downward path that is alcoholism. He has been sober several weeks. All three, weak in themselves, know that in the group alone lies their strength, and they have gathered again to share it.

Long weeks at sea in a submarine can be trying to any man. Restlessness grows: nerves are on edge; well-intentioned words can lead to anger; the strongest of men can become irritated over a spilled cup of coffee or a stubbed toe. Were these feelings permitted to grow, they could be disastrous to an alcoholic trying to maintain his sobriety. But these three have their quiet meetings, twice weekly.

Each meeting helps to renew their emotional stability; each meeting strengthens the wall between past and present; and each meeting adds one more beam to the structure of once-shattered lives being rebuilt.

There is a power greater than ourselves which makes this rebuilding possible and it is present, even beneath the sea.

*Bill O.*
*Key West, Florida*

# How Deep Does Your Sobriety Go?
November 1994

I am a sailor on a submarine here on the East Coast. I went through treatment in San Diego in 1980 at the Navy's request. I believed I was an alcoholic, but I didn't think that I needed AA after treatment, although I always carried a meeting schedule for the area where I was stationed in case anything went wrong.

I went on OK without a drink until 1988. That year everything that could go wrong did go wrong, until I finally succumbed to my disease and got drunk shortly before the end of the year. I'd been warned in treatment that should I choose to pick up a drink again, I would be right back where I had left off. Eight years dry hadn't slowed my drinking down at all. I am a blackout drinker and a couple of hours after I started drinking again I blacked out. When I came to, the stark reality hit me like a cold shower: if I didn't get back to AA, I might never get another chance.

My first year back in the Fellowship was a roller coaster ride. I was all over the place. I got first one sponsor, then another. I began to pick up ashtrays, put away chairs, and take out the trash. I made coffee, chaired meetings, and drove a group from a detox to a meeting once a week. I was determined to stay sober at all costs. I spent more time listening than I had done during any time in my life. I didn't start feeling great right away, but I did feel better. But there was one area I was vulnerable in, and before long I was in a relationship—with a baby on the way to boot. My sponsor said that he would see me through if I made up my mind to stay in the relationship, even though we both knew what it could do to my sobriety if things went sour. My girlfriend and I had a lot of support since we were both in the program, and before long we were married and I had orders to go on sea duty aboard the Navy's newest fast-attack submarine. Things went well even though I was at sea most of the time. There was no AA person to talk to on my ship so I got the next best thing—I took a lot of AA books and tapes and read and prayed as often as I could.

One day while we were submerged at sea, the message came that my wife had been taken to the hospital and had given birth to our son; they were both in guarded condition. A relief was on the way to replace me so I could go back. This meant only one thing. Something had gone wrong and I wasn't getting the whole story. Having been around the Navy for a while, I knew that either my wife or my son was not out of danger. I was sickened.

Before I could even grasp what was happening, my disease resurfaced with all the fury of a hurricane. Without a penny in my pocket, I was already figuring out how I could get drunk either at the airport or on the plane ride back. I had no one to talk to and I was scared to death to make the flight alone for fear that if I started drinking, I wouldn't get back to AA. Then and there I was brought to my knees. My battle against my Higher Power was over without even a fight. I prayed only for his will and not mine and to accept whatever should happen. I was still shaky but at least I was functional. Gradually a couple more messages arrived, and I put together bits and pieces and came to the conclusion that it was my son who was worse off. Then I learned that his condition had reversed and both he and my loving wife were out of danger. I would stay aboard after all, as they were well taken care of.

I have fought God all my life. He knew of no other way to get me to Step Three than to bring it home to my doorstep. I once saw the following saying: "Alcoholism is the two-by-four that God used to get my attention." Today my faith in my Higher Power is my greatest asset in AA. Learning to let go and let God has become my greatest strength.

I will be returning to sea aboard the submarine, and as far as I know there will be no other AAs on board. But I know what to do and no matter what happens, even below the waves, my Higher Power will stand his silent vigil over me as long as I let him.

*Rick S.*
*Groton, Connecticut*

## Sober Sailor

*(From: Dear Grapevine)*
August 1961

I still live from day to day in the old 24-hour way, and it is wonderful. Many of the people in the Navy are quite surprised that I am not drinking, and I think they have adopted a wait-and-see attitude. One nice thing, though, is that none of my old chums has insisted that I have a drink. They are probably too shocked to speak.

I avoid the chief's club unless I have an absolute reason for being there because I believe that there is no use tempting fate. I've made it known that I've joined AA, as this generally reduces the number of hecklers and also there might be someone in the crowd who could be looking for help. I have some literature which I brought with me from Nova Scotia.

I've had a talk with the town padre, and I've been thinking about talking with the police and the hospital up here. I might just be lucky enough to find a kindred spirit and get a group started. Wouldn't that be wonderful for me?

In lieu of meetings, I've taken to attending church. I was never particularly interested before, but I approach it with an open mind. If I like what the padre says, I accept. If not, I reject. This way it gives me food for thought and keeps my mind on healthy things.

*G. T. B.*
*Inuvik, Northwest Territories*

## Staying Afloat
April 1988

I had been in the Navy for two years when I found out I was an alcoholic. It seems only fitting that I ended up there just as the Navy was going through its own "spiritual awakening." Before my time the Navy would have given the alcoholic an undesirable discharge. But they had discovered that the alcoholic could be saved and made whole again. In my own eyes, though, I had become the worst thing in the world that one could be—an alcoholic. And at 22 years of age, to boot

It happened in Charleston, South Carolina, on a ship. I had drunk myself into such a state that the people around me decided I should be helped—and held accountable for my actions. Drunk on duty again, mouthy to anyone who would listen, pranks pulled while drunk, sick for days after my drunks, not able to put in a full day's work without becoming thirsty for one beer, maybe two or three, and then off again. The same story ever since high school.

I was allowed to have alcohol at a very young age at home. My first drink was served to me in a tall stem glass. It bubbled and tasted real good. It made me feel good too, and I wanted more, but more than one or two glasses I was not allowed to have. On weekends my father would take me with him to the local bar and grill so he could hoist a few. I would play shuffleboard with the dimes I was given, and a few sips from Dad's beer were absolute heaven. Between that time and the time I graduated from high school, I took a drink every time it presented itself.

I was allowed to drink at home, in fact my mother would buy it for me—so I wouldn't drink and drive, she said. By the time I was 18, I was the class beer buyer in high school. Beer was it for me, but cherry vodka was cool at dances. One could smell the cherries, and others would know I was drinking and therefore cool. When I was drunk I felt I was a better lover, a better liar, a bigger person, the life and soul of the party. I could be any person I wanted to be. My mother and father had divorced when I was 12, and I always felt less than everyone else who had a normal family. I became known as "Uncle Bud" to the class of 71.

I went off to attend a college to study fishing (oceanography) for two years. There, in the South, I was arrested for the first time for being drunk in public, and for writing bad checks to get money to drink with. I fell in with a crowd that liked to drink, raise hell, and drink again. There were campus parties all the time. My grades were so-so, and I had no goals for the future. It was all just one big play time.

After the two years were up I moved back up North to stay with my dad, whom I hadn't seen in years. The change in location didn't help the way I felt or the way I drank. Dad and I would pop a few together while fishing in the boat, or at the local tavern.

But when I went out by myself, I always came home drunk. I never knew how many I would have, or when to stop. I now started to drink for a reason: I didn't like myself. I was unhappy about my broken family, I had no job, and I felt that I just wasn't good enough. I couldn't stop.

A crazy stunt I used to pull was to ride up and down the local highway and play police officer. I drove a VW Beetle on which I fixed a flasher so that I could pull people over. With my short hair and the Merchant Marine identification card I had from being on the ships at school, I looked somewhat official. With the light flashing, I would pull people over to the side of the road for speeding and give them a verbal warning. All the time, I was blasted out of my mind and in and out of blackouts. Once I put the name of a person on a real warning ticket I had. He turned out to be the commander of a nearby training school for the armed services. He sent my name into the draft board to tell them that I was no longer in school.

I had no place to go, and there was no work to be found. I enlisted the next week to keep from being drafted. There I found good food, money every two weeks to drink with, and a place to rest. Also, my stepmother had asked me one morning while I was throwing up if my drinking was a problem. I had moved out into my own apartment, but I had lost that too. I was losing everything around me, and the Navy looked real good.

They took me as an E-3, with two years of college. I was the company first platoon leader, as I was the oldest in the group. I made out the watch bill so I could sleep at night and do less work. When boot camp was over, I picked up my drinking where I had left off 12 weeks earlier, but I was telling so many lies now that trouble started to follow me everywhere I went. But now there was a difference. I was no longer the 95-pound weakling I had been. I was a well-trained fighting man who had a hatred for the world and a chip on my shoulder. Drunk, I became brave, and fights were common with me. One night I got badly beaten up at a bar, and I volunteered for extra training to really learn how to fight. I was dangerous.

I was sent to the fleet, and attached to a ship that was going places: the Mediterranean, the Caribbean, Turkey, France and Italy. Every port we pulled into, I was drunk within the hour.

One night when I was drunk on duty for the umpteenth time, the Navy stepped in. I was sent to the local Navy hospital for rehabilitation. At the unit, as we called it, I was introduced to AA. We were taken by van to local meetings, and I felt good around those people. I fitted in. I fitted in more than with my own family back home, and I wanted more of this.

When we got to port, I wasn't allowed to leave the ship because the watch bill had been made out and I wasn't on it. I was so angry, I lost my temper with the deck officer, and grabbed him like a piece of ham.

I beat him up, and I was arrested and put in jail. I was so out of touch that at the court martial I thought I heard them say 28 years in the brig. My heart sank. All my problems until now seemed like nothing, and I felt hopeless. I was certain that I was never going to get better.

One night in my cell, I did something that I vowed I would never do. I asked God, as I understood him, for help. I had vowed I would never do that, as I felt that it was his fault that I was in jail in the first place, that everything had been his fault. But here I was with all hope gone, and I turned to him for an answer. There was no flash of light such as Bill W. mentioned in the Big Book, but a feeling of willingness and well-being began to creep over me. Before, there had only been loneliness.

Twenty days later I was set free on good behavior, and that night I was at an AA meeting. Later that month I started my Fourth Step, soon to be followed by my Fifth. I began to ask God what to do, and any desire to return to drinking was gone. A year later, I was honorably discharged.

It has now been 12 years for me without a drink in Alcoholics Anonymous. I found myself another home group and began to clean ashtrays, make coffee and get involved with the whole program. I still do the very same things I did when I was new. I have served as a general service representative for my group, and have grown from the experience. I was elected to be my district's representative to our area assembly, and while I was on the committee, they asked me to be their treasurer. It has been a fast journey for me since I got here. There is still more to do for the still-suffering alcoholic, and still more for me to do. I came to find that I need the newcomer more than he/she needs me, and that I must give this away if I intend to stay sober.

I still have a home group. I am still a sponsor, and I still make the coffee. I thank God for AA, and I thank AA for my God. Action was the magic word for me, and when in trouble I use the Twelfth Step, and my trouble eases as I help another.

AA has been like a flashlight in the night for me, a place where I always want to be. But I had to put the unusable oars in the water and pull out the spiritual ideas I didn't believe in. As I did my ship's bow appeared and I am getting where I am going, one day at a time.

*Bill S.*
*Pittsford, New York*

## AA Underwater
*(From: Dear Grapevine)*
April 2007

**A**fter a few months of sobriety and a 28-day treatment program, I was deployed on a U.S. nuclear submarine. We would be out for three months at a time. I was scared and brought all of my AA literature.

To my surprise, there were two other AA members onboard. So, we started a group. Once a week, we would sit in the library and have a meeting. I was able to stay focused on one day at a time a few hundred feet under the North Atlantic Ocean. I am eternally grateful for that meeting and those AA shipmates.

That was 30 years ago and by the grace of God and the Fellowship of AA, I am sober and still attend AA meetings.

*Anonymous*

## Danger: Port Ahead
August 2015

**I** was just under two years sober and 23 years old, when the Twin Towers in New York were hit. I was serving on base security at the time, and I knew everything would be different from then on out. Four months later, I was transferred to a small ship during the initial push for Operation Enduring Freedom. We deployed in January of 2002 and I quickly found myself surrounded by lots of drinking and no other AA members onboard. My sponsor, also a Navy man, was deployed as well, but not on my ship. Communications with my AA family became non-existent (small ships did not have phones or reliable internet at that time.) So God, AA speaker tapes, my Big Book, and Grapevines I received from my home group members (just like AAs did during WWII) became my program for the next six months.

After three months, we pulled into port with the NATO fleet and I desperately wanted to get off the ship. However, the Navy policy requires a "buddy" system when on deployment so no one goes out in town alone. I did the best I could in selecting shipmates who would be "safe," and we set out into town to "watch a movie and get something to eat." However, somewhere along the way two of the guys said, "Let's stop by the bar and have a beer." Just for the record, if a sailor says, "Let's get a beer," he is lying through his teeth. Eight hours later we were still at that bar! I couldn't leave my buddies (or we'd get in trouble) so I stayed there and drank all the soda in the bar (OK, I'm exaggerating, not all). But I did carry a cup in my hand all the time, ate the food, played pool and did all the sober "tricks" I had learned to use when in party situations.

However, alcoholism is cunning—and slick. It doesn't come at us head on, but always from the side. Just like that, a man placed a glass of ale in front of me. Hmm ... I had never had ale. It was red and looked fruity. I thought, That looks like it tastes good ... I want to taste it. Baffling! I didn't want to lose my career and the blessings of two years of sobriety, or hurt those I love. I just wanted to "taste" the ale. Luckily, the blessing of the Second Step instantly began to materialize. I heard in my head voices of AA members and quotes from the Big Book: "To drink is to die," "It's the first drink that gets you drunk." I knew I was in danger.

Yet those words didn't break the compulsion to taste the ale. The Big Book states: "The alcoholic at certain times has no effective mental defense against the first drink. Except in a few rare cases, neither he nor any other human being can provide such a defense. His defense must come from a Higher Power." This was that certain time, and no mental defense seemed to be working.

I've never been a fan of the expression "Meeting makers make it." I've seen many "meeting makers" who don't establish a relationship with a power greater than themselves, get drunk. The meetings don't actually keep me sober, but they do offer me an opportunity to gain a better relationship with my God and his kids. I guess the real expression should be "Meeting makers make it possible to make it." Thanks to going to lots of meetings, I had heard someone say, "If you're at a party and you feel squirrelly, go to the bathroom and pray." Well, I was feeling squirrelly, and being on my knees in a bathroom had been second nature during my drinking; so, by God's grace, off to the bathroom I went to seek guidance and assistance from a power greater than myself.

I returned to the table and the compulsion remained, so I returned to the bathroom a second time and prayed to God to help me stay sober. Then the compulsion was removed. I left that bar free from the consequences of a drink, and I was able to finish that deployment sober (eventually hitting a meeting in Norway). I returned to my home group armed not with the knowledge that God would keep them sober, but with the knowledge that God would keep me sober, because he had.

I completed a second deployment after that. The same thing happened in Panama when I was four and a half years sober and I had to do the same "bathroom prayer" again. I got the same results. I'm now a 36-year-old veteran with 14 years of sobriety. By God's grace, I hope that if the compulsion ever returns, I'll continue to have the willingness to use the bathroom prayer so God can restore me to sanity again.

*Aaron N.*
*Abbott, Texas*

## Submarine Sobriety
*(From: From the Grass Roots)*
June 1960

We have a group meeting regularly at the Naval Base here. Had our fourth weekly meeting last night, and the group is coming along much better than expected. In three weeks we've attracted seven new members. Several Navy Chaplains, two Navy doctors, the Base Commanding Officer, and several other high brass have become interested since we began in November.

They are cooperating much more than we could have hoped for. I've been trying for almost three years to get a group aboard a Navy base so I imagine you can guess how I feel.

I'm so glad now that I didn't get discouraged and give up because, although it is the first, I know it won't be long before we have one on every Navy base throughout the world. As you know we cracked the ice with the "Dolphin" group aboard the submarine I was on last year, which is still active in Key West but merged with a civilian group there. Anyway, we've made a beginning and that's all it takes.

Our whole sub squadron was transferred here in July. I miss the Key West group but also had many AA friends here, and now have many more.

*B. O.*
*Charleston, South Carolina*

## And Then We Were Five

February 1976

'm in the Canadian Navy and at the moment part of a NATO squadron. Ships from the Navies of Canada, England, the Netherlands, Norway, West Germany, and the U.S. are pooled in this squadron. We visit different countries in Europe, showing the NATO flag.

Having been the only AA member on board for the past two years, I found it was a must for me, at times, to get in contact with AA members in these ports to keep my sanity. The most delightful occasion came when we arrived in Chatham, England, for a three-week visit. As soon as the ship was tied up, I was on my way to the England and Wales Convention in Selsey. This brought back the high we hear about so often after these gatherings of experience, strength, and hope. But the best was yet to come, and it was almost as baffling as alcohol.

Most of the ship's company is aware that I'm a member of AA, and some have asked me questions or have asked to read the Big Book, with this final result: "It's good for you, Art, but I don't think I'm that bad yet."

A shipmate who sleeps in the same mess that I do had been deteriorating very rapidly (from bunk to drink to bunk, etc.). Being on duty on Sunday, he had to come out into view of civilization, and it was noticed by all that he was unfit for duty. He was admitted to sick bay. The following morning, I was asked if I would see Sid, because he was interested in what AA could do for him. So I had my first Twelfth Step call on this trip, and that night, Sid and I went to a meeting. On Monday, there were two of us.

A couple of days prior to this, the medical assistant (Bob) was approached by a fellow who said he was becoming very depressed and mentioned he had attended some AA meetings back home in Halifax. Bob asked if I had any suggestions. Bob himself had approached me about AA at one time, and I had given him literature, but he had changed his mind the next day. This time, I couldn't give him enough to read. Tuesday morning, Bob said, "I would like to join your organization." On Tuesday, there were three of us.

Harry, the fellow with the depressions, had an appointment to see Bob on Wednesday at 10:00 AM. When Harry came into sick bay, Bob opened the top drawer of his desk, pointed at some AA literature, and said, "This is what you need."

Harry said, "OK." On Wednesday, there were four of us.

Thursday morning, I was approached by Jim, and he said he'd like to speak to me. I took him up to my office, and he gave me a story about having broken into the captain's cabin to steal booze and having been caught by the captain. Surprisingly, the captain didn't punish him, but said he needed help (this wasn't Jim's first time) and sent him to talk with Bob, who in turn sent him to me. On Thursday night, when we went to the meeting in Gillingham, England, there were five of us.

The previous Thursday, I had been at that same meeting by myself and had told the local members that I'd been the only member aboard for the past two years. To show up with four other members the following Thursday was unreal!

Many members say, "It keeps getting better," and that's true. Just ask me.

*Art C.*
*Dartmouth, Nova Scotia*

## My People!

*(From: Dear Grapevine)*
October 1981

I came into AA through the Navy's Alcoholic Rehabilitation Program (for which I'm very grateful). From treatment, I was sent back to my duty station at Andrews Air Force Base and became a member of the AA group there.

When leave came around, I was scared that I wouldn't find the kind of people that I knew at Andrews while I was home in West Virginia. Well, a few days after I arrived, the AA members started calling me every day, and I went to meetings every day. I grew to love them all very much. They made it easy for me to adjust. One guy was from Washington and knew a lot of the AA people that I knew in D.C. He became my West Virginia sponsor.

Later, I was transferred to ship duty in Florida, and I started getting some of the same scared feelings. When I arrived, I met up with a friend from D.C., went to a lot of meetings with him, and asked him to be my Florida sponsor. I later met another guy from Washington, two girls here on vacation, one of whom had been to my home group at Andrews several times, and then a couple on vacation from D.C. who had recently spoken at my home group.

I hope that I'll never feel that uneasiness again, but if I do, I know that the God of my understanding will see to it that the right people are put into my life—AA people. My people!

*C. F.*
*Mayport, Florida*

# Fair Winds and Following Seas
May 2005

I was raised in a small town in Mississippi. The town itself was somewhat storybook fashion, in the sense that everyone knew everyone else, got involved in each other's lives and genuinely cared for one another. Friday night high school football was an all-hands evolution (as we say in military life). It was a very close-knit community. Looking back, it was a great place to call home.

During my high school years, however, no one could have convinced me that there was anything positive about my home town. I was restless, irritable and discontented, and felt a need to escape. It wasn't the town itself I was running from as much as the home life. I was very sure our home was different from others in the dark of night, behind closed doors. It was, I now know, the typical environment created by the abuse of alcohol. By 1973, my mother's addiction to alcohol resulted in her suicide. I was 15 years old, and this deeply affected me. I was her biggest enabler, protector and caretaker. I could not understand how she could allow alcohol to destroy her life, as well as those who loved her, the way she did. That would never happen to me.

Three years and two stepmothers later, when I was graduating, I noticed everyone in my class seemed to have a plan for the future. I had no plan and was unwilling to ask for help. My father strongly suggested I consider the Navy, as he had. Not wanting his advice anymore, I was determined to make my own decisions. I knew I could do better. I joined the United States Coast Guard and left for basic training 10 days later. Little did I know this decision would save my life.

My first assignment after graduation from boot camp was as a cutter in Honolulu, Hawaii. I was introduced to a life I never imagined. Alcohol flowed freely and seemed to be the reward for a job well done. I was blessed with the ability to handle quantities of booze that only seasoned sailors at the time would dare attempt. According to my way of thinking (something I now call insanity), this defined me as the man I wanted to be, someone who was respected and looked up to. In my case, it was for my exceptional drinking abilities. It seemed I had chosen the perfect career and I was going places.

The routine lasted for 15 years, one duty station after another. There were the usual scrapes and close calls along the way, but never anything I couldn't find a way out of. After all, I was a top performer: I was always on time for work and had excellent performance marks—so far.

This, of course, didn't last. I began drinking daily, including on the job. At this point, I was living with that fear that only an alcoholic understands. The feelings of impending doom were constant. I was terrified of getting in trouble at work, yet I drank on the job daily. I knew the end was near when I began drinking on the ride to work in the morning—just to settle the nerves and gain the courage to face another day.

I should mention that I am in food service (the long way of saying I'm a cook) and required to be at work very early. Drinking en route to work, I realized that this was becoming a problem. I was not the hard-working, hard-drinking sailor people looked up to. I had a secret now that no one would find respectable. Instead of being the man and sailor I intended to be, I was growing farther and farther away with every drink. I was filled with what our book calls incomprehensible demoralization, yet I could do nothing to stop. I was drinking to forget about how much I drank yesterday.

The Coast Guard is a life-saving service, and sometimes they have to save their own. They did just that for me in 1992. After being two hours late for work for the third day in a row, I was arrested and sentenced to a Navy alcohol rehabilitation center in Norfolk, Virginia. I was there for six weeks, and during that time, met people who I'm convinced were not from this earth. They knew how I felt. They explained why I drank. For the first time, I knew I was not alone with my fears of living. They all seemed like angels. I felt safe, and somehow they broke down enough of my fears and misconceptions on life to allow a bit of hope to filter in. They gave me a solution by introducing me to the Twelve Steps of Alcoholics Anonymous, a God of my understanding, and a way of life I never would have imagined, along with the greatest gift of all—the people of Alcoholics Anonymous.

I realize today I had a Higher Power working in my life long before the United States Coast Guard and AA introduced us. I feel I have lived two lives. During my Coast Guard career, in my so-called first life, I traveled around the world drunk, seeing nothing and learning nothing. In 1992, I was given the tools I need to start the trip over again, in sobriety.

We AA members of all the armed forces should be very grateful for the long-reaching arms of AA worldwide. I have never been sent anywhere in my sober career where I haven't found a meeting of Alcoholics Anonymous. For guys like me who can sometimes find themselves far from home and in a lonely state of mind, an AA meeting always gives me that same safe feeling I had in the beginning of my sobriety in that Navy rehab. I am forever grateful to the people of AA who came before me, and I strive to continue to carry the message and be available for those hard-drinking sailors of the future.

I am still today an active duty chief petty officer with 25 years of service, hoping to complete a full 30 years. I am currently stationed at the Coast Guard recruit training center in Cape May, New Jersey. What does the Coast Guard trust a guy with my shady past to do with their new recruits? I teach substance abuse prevention, of course. It is the most rewarding job I have ever had or could imagine having. I am very grateful to the Coast Guard for their help, understanding and trust in me. Miracles do happen in sobriety if you just don't give up. What a gift this job is! Each of these new Coast Guard recruits must decide for themselves which road they wish to take. For those who will certainly take the rough way, I pray that we all do our part to make sure there is a safe place for them, as there was for me.

I am a member in good standing of the Saturday Night Live Group in Onancock, Virginia. We meet at 7:30 and if you are ever in the area, I know you, too, would feel safe there.

Fair winds and following seas.

*Tom W.*
*Pungoteague, Virginia*

CHAPTER FIVE

# Over There

AA members share about being stationed overseas, in faraway
places, often at war

T he stories in this chapter recount the efforts that AA members
have gone to to stay sober, often during wartime in unfamil-
iar places and extreme circumstances around the world.

In "Foxhole Fellowship," a story from 2008, Dave W. is a naval officer deployed to Baghdad, Iraq. He recounts how his AA group, which
met in a trailer inside the U.S. Embassy compound, had taken "rocket
fire." One explosion "shook everything down to my fillings," he writes.
The group members quickly scattered, seeking cover. When they recon-
vened after the "all clear sounded," the members resumed their meeting,
their hands still shaking when they joined hands for the Lord's Prayer.

In the story "Sober in Singapore," member G.A. of Chesapeake, Virginia is on a U.S. Navy ship that arrives in Singapore after months at
sea. He wanders the city "hungry, angry, lonely and tired." He calls a
local number in the International AA Directory—and is quickly introduced to a fellow AA staying in his hotel and an English-speaking AA
group. "That directory in my pocket," he writes, "was my key to much
AA fellowship, even in far-off Singapore."

"Staying Sober in the Sand" is a fascinating account from 2005
by Bill S. of Kingston, Ontario of his career as UN peacekeeper for
the Canadian Forces. While stationed on the Syrian side of the Golan
Heights, he had to make a tense border-crossing into Israel every Friday night to attend a meeting. "Through AA and God, I am now about
to celebrate my 26-year anniversary," he writes.

In the story "Put Our Your Hand," member B.H. of Fairfield, California shipped out to Goose Bay, Canada. He had to take an airplane

to reach the nearest AA meeting. "I have met loners and small groups all over the Far East and the Far North," he writes. "The welcome you get is out of this world ... You never have to be alone if you don't want to be."

## Staying Sober in the Sand
May 2005

I n 1996, after 19 years of sobriety, I was called in as a peacekeeper in the Golan Heights for the Canadian Forces. This was my second United Nations tour sober. My first one was in Cyprus in 1981 with five years of sobriety. I did one tour in Egypt in 1973 before finding the program of Alcoholics Anonymous and it was extremely dangerous—not the war-torn situation, but my drinking. It was dangerous to me and everyone else.

Before going to the Golan Heights, we went to St.-Jean, Quebec for 10 days to prepare for the tour. While there, I tried to find out if anyone was a friend of Bill W.'s. However, no one came forward. After I arrived in Israel, I contacted the doctor at the camp, and he gave me the name of a fellow who had been there for three months and was looking for a member or a meeting.

Unfortunately, I soon found out that I was going to the Syrian side and he would be on the Israeli side; therefore it would be hard for us to get together for a meeting. However, once I found out his name and work phone number I gave him a call. He had a small group going on the other side, and he was eager to find a new member. There were three of them—two guys and a girl. I was excited about finding three other members.

After my first week of work, I put in for a pass to go over to the Israeli side for a Friday night meeting that my contact had planned. After the red tape of border-crossings manned first by Syrian soldiers and then by Israeli soldiers, I made it to the Canadian camp. I finally found my contact and knew one of the other fellows from a meeting I had attended years before in Borden. That day was the girl's three-year birthday and we were all going out to dinner in nearby Tiberius.

What a time we had! We had a meeting afterward with a birthday cake. I went over to the Israeli side every Friday for three months until those AAs left, and then I became a loner again. I contacted the doctor but no one was a friend of Bill W.'s on the new rotation.

When I was working with the Austrians on the Syrian side, I asked the priest if he knew of any alcoholics working there. Something must have gone wrong in the translation because his reply was, "We had one here, but we sent him home right away." He also had never heard of Alcoholics Anonymous. There were many drunks getting into a lot of trouble in the camp.

I continued to read my Big Book daily and I dropped into the church every day to say my daily prayers and do my meditation. Then I went home for my leave to celebrate my 20th year of sobriety. I was more excited about celebrating than I was about going home for my son's wedding. However, everything turned out beautifully. I had an excellent 20-year celebration and my son's wedding was not bad either.

I then returned to the Golan Heights for another six weeks of no meetings. I wrote to New York to obtain an AA contact over there, but none were available. I did receive a nice letter from the General Service Office though, congratulating me on 20 years of sobriety.

There were drinking parties every night. I watched people being taken to the hospital after falling down and hitting the rocks after too many drinks. Two soldiers in my detachment were involved in a drunken brawl and one received a broken jaw. Over that fight, I lost both men, one to the hospital and the other to jail for 30 days and then to the rehab.

I kept busy trying to stay in shape, praying a lot and reading the Big Book. I also wrote to many AA members back in Canada and I received a lot of support from them. I would even spend the money to call one particular AA member when I got real stressed out. I knew it would be a lot cheaper than picking up a drink. Through AA and God, I am now about to celebrate my 26-year anniversary.

*Bill S.*
*Kingston, Ontario*

## Finding Fellowship

June 1997

I n the spring of 1990, as a member of the Canadian Air Force, I was on a joint military exercise with some members of the U.S. Navy in Thule, Greenland. My part in the exercise meant I'd be in Thule for two to three weeks. Being the only recovering alcoholic on the crew, and having only a few months of sobriety, I began looking for an AA meeting as soon as I was on the ground. At that time Thule had a contingent of U.S. Air Force personnel in place; so I started with the Air Force police. A helpful policeman recalled there had been a meeting in the past, but thought it was now shut down. Someone else confirmed that no regular meeting was held on the base.

Having no hope of finding an English-speaking meeting near the base, I set about finding another AA member. Our living accommodations were in barrack blocks, which we shared with Navy personnel. Although there were enough recreation facilities, most included or were centered around a bar service and held little attraction for me. In our barracks there were two TV rooms, one on the second floor where the Canadians watched the Stanley Cup playoffs each night, and another on the first floor, near my room, where the Americans watched movies.

One night in the first-floor TV room, one sailor asked another why he didn't stay long at the TOW (Top of the World) Club, which was a bar and restaurant. The sailor (I'll call him John) said, "When you don't smoke or drink, that place doesn't offer much." This answer caught my ear and before leaving the room, I took a good look at the fellow. The next evening, I saw him and a friend come into the theater lobby where I was in the admission line. It was a long line because it was also for beer. I asked John if I could speak to him for a moment and then led him to a far corner where we could not be overheard. I asked him if I'd heard correctly what he'd said about the TOW Club, and then I asked if he was a friend of Bill W. His whole face lit up and with a beaming smile he introduced himself as a recovering alcoholic. We arranged to meet after the movie and we shared some of our experience, strength and hope. Neither of us felt tempted to drink, but we were both happy to find fellowship where no meetings were available. During the rest of my time in Thule, John and I didn't have an actual AA meeting, but our almost daily contact gave me a sense of security. (And when I finished reading my current Grapevine, John was glad to have it.)

I often think of John and hope he's doing well. When people in a meeting speak of going to any length to stay sober, I get the mental picture of a beaming smile on the face of a recovering alcoholic in Thule, Greenland.

*Anonymous*
*Moose Jaw, Saskatchewan*

## Sober in Singapore
March 1982

A merican Navy ships began making regular port calls in Singapore early in 1980. On two different port calls, I was received very warmly by the AA group there. On the first, it was amazing to discover AA alive and well in such a far-off place.

It took us six and a half hours to get a liberty boat ride ashore. It was hot and humid, and we'd been at sea for 94 days straight. Emotions were running high, as most of the talk for weeks had concerned beer and ladies. I had not had any AA fellowship since leaving Norfolk, Virginia, except for Grapevine and material I receive as an AA Internationalist. I had wanted to just relax in a hotel, but when I tried one after another, I found they were full, mostly with sailors from the American battle group.

Well, I was hungry, angry, lonely and tired. Even after two years of sobriety, when I passed a sign showing a large mug of frosty beer, it looked mighty good. At that moment, probably the only thing that stood between me and that first drink was my God, as I understand him. Earlier in the day, fortunately, I had placed a copy of the International AA Directory in my pocket. As I looked at that picture of beer, I felt the directory. Walking into a nearby hotel, I dialed the Singapore number listed in the directory and got the local group's recording. "Leave your telephone number," it said. The only number I had was for the hotel I was calling from. I gave that, after asking the desk clerk if he would page me in the hotel restaurant.

Suddenly, events began to take a turn for the better. The clerk inquired if I was an American sailor, saying that the major hotels in town were offering us a 10 percent discount and that they still had rooms available.

The phone was ringing in my room as I walked in. The gentleman on the phone introduced himself and said that I would shortly get a call from another person, who could speak better English. Actually, his voice sounded wonderful after so many months of no contact with another AA. We spoke for several more minutes, and I told him how badly I needed a meeting and how close I had come to that first drink.

About an hour later, I received a call from a woman AA, a British citizen living in Singapore. She gave me directions to the AA meeting place and offered to give me a ride if necessary. She also gave me the name and room number of an American AA who was staying in the same hotel as me. The meeting was the next night, so I looked up the AA in my hotel, and we had our own mini-meeting that very night.

At the meeting the following night, I received many invitations to dinner and offers to show me the city—so typical of AA fellowship anywhere. The meeting itself was an international experience. There were Indians, Americans, British, Australians, Malaysians, New Zealanders, French, and Chinese. Singapore is a tourist city and also has many international business corporations.

That directory in my pocket was my key to much AA fellowship, even in far-off Singapore.

*G. A.*
*Chesapeake, Virginia*

## Thanks for Another "Coincidence"

*(From: Dear Grapevine)*
April 1984

Since April 25, 1982, there have been United States soldiers in the Southern Sinai to guarantee the peace treaty between Egypt and Israel. I have been here in the desert since August 1982 and finally found two other members of the Fellowship with whom to hold meetings. A third one joined us a little later; that made four altogether. In February, the other three left because their tour was up, so there I was, a loner again.

Early in March, I was sitting in the dining facility one evening with a fellow from Ohio, who introduced another Ohioan across the table. I mentioned that the only really significant event in Ohio history must have been the meeting of two men, back in 1935, who went on to found a worldwide fellowship. "You mean AA?" said the man across the table. It turned out that he was in AA and looking for a meeting. He also knew another member, so now the Sharm al-Sheikh group is continuing, thanks to one of those "coincidences" that happen so often in AA.

*F. K.*
*Sharm al-Sheikh, Egypt*

## Soldier Down

October 2011

I woke up and saw the clock—5:02 A.M. I had to be in formation at 5:30. I think I had stopped drinking and gone to bed around 1 A.M. What a way to start a Monday, I thought as I stumbled into the bathroom. Usually I would take a quick shower after a night of

heavy drinking, but not today. I didn't have time. I got dressed and
ran out to the car and drove off toward the post.

I arrived at the formation just in time. Within a couple minutes, my
platoon sergeant called me to the side. "How much did you drink last
night?" she asked. "What do you mean?" I said.

Responding in a hushed but stern voice, she told me that I reeked
like a brewery. She said that if we went to the military police station
at that very moment, a breathalyzer would show that I was over the
limit and I'd be considered drunk on duty. "So I am going to ask you
one more time. How much did you drink last night?" she repeated. "I
really don't know, Sergeant. I can't remember."

It was over. Years of hiding my drinking and staying off the blotter
report had come to a sudden and crushing end. Fifteen years of my
military career were slipping away from me! I would be kicked out
and disgraced. As I stood there thinking of all the possible things that
could happen, she looked at me and said, "Thank you for being honest. We'll talk about this later."

I sobered up at work and at the end of the work day she called me
into her office. "Shut the door and sit down, Sergeant," she said. "What
I am going to say is to stay in this room, do you understand?" Knowing
that the hammer was about to drop, I agreed. But it wasn't the hammer that I was expecting. "I have suspected for a while that you may
have been hiding your drinking, but until today I couldn't prove it. I
am concerned that you may have a problem with alcohol. I would like
you to report to the Army Substance Abuse Program. Also, as a member of AA, I would like to invite you to a meeting tonight with me."

I was shocked! Where were the terrible consequences I had imagined? Where was the notification that I had violated the Uniform
Code of Military Justice? Where was the axe to end my career? She
could have done all of that and more, but instead she was asking me
to seek help and inviting me to an AA meeting. What a deal!

So of course I agreed, and that night went to my first AA meeting.
When I sat down, an older man named Lou asked, "So what brings
you here?" I started to say, "Well, a lot of little things that culminated

in ... " He stopped me in mid-sentence, "This program is based on honesty. If you can't be honest with yourself, then this program won't work for you." How right he was! I honestly wanted to get the "problem" fixed, so I could go back to the way things were. I didn't think I was an alcoholic, but I listened to Lou share his story along with several others that night. I picked up a 24-hour chip and didn't drink for the rest of the week, until Friday night when back to the bottle I went.

I thought that if going to a few meetings a week would save me from getting kicked out of the Army, then it was a small price to pay. So, I kept my agreement and I went to the substance abuse program. I also told my wife that I had to work late on the nights I went to meetings with my supervisor. For about two months I showed up regularly to the meetings, but I continued to drink. The only thing that changed was that I tried to hide my drinking even more. I went to AA because I wanted my supervisor to see me at a meeting once or twice a week so she would think I was working on my drinking problem. While I was there, I did listen to people sharing their stories and discussed the selected readings, but I just didn't think that it applied much to me. Well, the only thing that changed was that I hid my drinking even more. But on Sunday, April 25, 2010, that all changed.

After working for most of the day in preparation for an upcoming inspection, I felt I deserved a couple of beers for all the hard work I had done on a day I would normally be off. So I stopped at the store on the way home and bought a full rack of German beer, intending to go home to have what I thought would be a beer or two at most. I had convinced myself that I didn't have a problem after all. I could stop drinking any time I wanted—I just didn't want to. I was standing on the balcony smoking a cigarette and drinking the sixth half-liter beer from that rack that I had bought just two hours earlier. This was the same balcony I had fallen off of eight months earlier in a drunken stupor that nearly cost me my life. Then suddenly, my 7-year-old daughter walked up and said, "Daddy, I don't want you to drink and die." I asked her what she had just said, and she repeated, "I don't want you to drink and drive." Drive? I thought she said "die." I know she said "die." I looked at my half-finished bottle of beer and the thought hit me like a ton of bricks: I can't stop drinking! If I don't stop, I'm going to die drunk!

I quietly walked over to the sink and for the first time in my 38 years of life, I poured out my beer. I stood there watching it flow down the drain and I felt an intense sense of relief. I seriously felt for the first time that maybe I really could stop. Maybe with the help of a Higher Power, I could change this fate of a drunken death. I went to the next AA meeting on Monday night and admitted to the group that I truly had become powerless over alcohol and that my life had honestly become unmanageable. I openly and honestly shared my story for the first time, and this soldier fell apart. The tears fell from my face as I received my second 24-hour chip.

Finally, I have seriously started to work the program of AA; I've begun my journey of sobriety! By putting the principles of AA into action, the first of which is honesty, I no longer lie to my wife that I'm working late. Instead, she knows I am going to AA meetings. In fact, she has attended some open meetings with me as well. I know that I am always just one drink away from my next drunk, and that I need to only focus on not drinking one day at a time. Because I have worked the program to the best of my abilities with my sponsor, I have been able to stay sober for a year now. I do this by making a daily commitment not to drink today, and I work the program for me.

Recently during a discussion of Step One in one of our Twelve and Twelve meetings, I read: "It is truly awful to admit that, glass in hand, we have warped our minds into such an obsession for destructive drinking that only an act of Providence can remove it from us." I have read the passage several times, but I felt I had to look up the word "providence" in the dictionary.

According to Webster, providence is divine guidance or care; God-conceived power sustaining and guiding human destiny. After reading this definition, another ton of bricks fell on me as I realized that I think I experienced an act of providence while I had my last drink in my hand. My daughter could have said, "drive," but I heard "die," and in that moment I came to believe that I was indeed an alcoholic and that AA does have the solution, and God has the power.

*David A.*
*Kaiserslautern, Germany*


# Foxhole Fellowship

*(From: Dear Grapevine)*
January 2008

I'm a naval officer currently deployed to Baghdad, Iraq. We have an active AA group here that meets in a trailer inside the U.S. Embassy compound.

During a meeting in June, we began to take rocket fire. They exploded around the compound and the resounding booms reverberated in our trailer.

One of the regulars, Rick, was sharing about his struggle with a bitter divorce when we heard the distinctive whistle of a rocket passing directly overhead. It struck, exploded about 100 feet from our trailer, and shook everything down to my fillings. We broke from the room—about a dozen of us—and scattered. Over the next several minutes, our group regathered in the closest bunker. A few non-alcoholics were there, so we AAs moved to one end and began talking to Rick, sharing our experience, strength, and hope in staying sober through divorce. He was not alone in his experience.

After a few minutes, the "all clear" sounded. We had nine minutes left in our hour, so we headed back to the trailer. When we joined hands for the Lord's Prayer, some hands shook from the fear and adrenaline of dodging rockets. We were all OK—just for that day. The prayer went up with a little more feeling than usual.

*Dave W.*

## Pressed Into Service

June 2003

When I first arrived on Okinawa, Japan, for duty with the Marine Corps, there was no meeting near the camp I lived on. I thought about starting one, but I never got around to acting on it. Once I got comfortable driving on Okinawa, I decided to check for meetings at the other camps and bases on the island. Then I found a meeting schedule for a group in the camp I work at and went to the Monday night meeting. When I got there, I discovered that the group no longer existed.

Not wanting to give up on the search for a meeting, I decided to give a Friday-night speaker meeting on the Air Force base a shot. Success! I decided I would start going to it regularly. But why were these people making so many comments about how the meetings at my camp died because there was no one to run them?

That got me thinking that maybe I should do it, but not enough to get me to commit. The following Monday, the substance-abuse counselor for my command approached me. He said there were a few Marines in the command who needed meetings, but there wasn't one on the camp anymore. Could I help out? Again, I started thinking maybe I should, but I was still a little deaf to God's voice.

On Tuesday, I went to the chapel where the meeting room was to see if the old group had left any information with the chaplain. That's when God got tired of me not listening and slapped me upside the head. The chapel was open, but there was no one inside. I looked in the meeting room, and there on the white board next to the old meeting schedule was a note from a Marine who had come to the chapel for a meeting on Saturday and found no one there. He was desperate enough to leave his name, rank, unit, and phone number on the board. "OK, Lord," I said. "I hear you."

I went back to my unit and found another sober alcoholic. We agreed that I would start a Monday night meeting, and he would do Wednesday. We also agreed to use our vehicles every Friday to shuttle as many people we could to the meeting at the Air Force base. Then I went to look for the Marine who wrote the note, and we had an impromptu meeting. I found one grateful alcoholic, and I believe I have a commitment from him to come to our new meetings.

*John F.*
*Okinawa, Japan*

## Put Out Your Hand
*(From: Carrying the Message)*
February 1966

I was in Korea in 1960 and helped to start a group there. I also saw AA in action in Japan. Then I was shipped to Vandenberg AFB in the fall and helped to start a group at that base. We were so small I was Secretary and GSR both. In 1962 I was shipped to Greenland for a few months, then near Goose Bay, Labrador. This place was out on a chain of very remote sites. It was the end of nowhere. I did get into Goose Bay by air at times and they had two meetings a week there, one American and one Canadian, but they were nearly one group, they were so close. This is the reason Grapevine means so much to me.

When I got back here in 1963 some guy at a meeting asked me how I stayed sober in a place like that. I told him I didn't drink. But also I told him of the help I had from different AA members whom I wrote to and was able to call on the phone (through what we called the hotline) to different Air Force bases who had AA members—also the help of Grapevine and World Services.

I have met loners and small groups all over the Far East and the Far North. The welcome you get is out of this world. They lay out the red carpet for you. You never have to be alone if you don't want to be. Sometimes you have to put out a little effort to find or contact some of these members, but it is sure worth it. I have been to many meetings in this country and around the world and they are all basically the same.

I have heard different ones say this group or that was not friendly, but I have not found this to be true. They will be just as friendly as you will let them be. Just don't be backward about putting out your hand.

*B. H.*
*Fairfield, California*

## My Alcoholism, My War

February 2002

I was a professional Army man, and a newcomer, when my country, Argentina, became embroiled in a border dispute and came close to going to war with Chile. I was stationed in Comodoro Rivadavia, and was sent to Río Turbio in the province of Santa Cruz, in the southernmost part of the continent.

I remember that all sections of my regiment had a mate kit. (Mate is a hot beverage brewed from a native shrub, popular in some Latin American countries. It is normally served in a hollowed-out gourd with a metal straw and is constantly refilled and passed around for sharing.) Our mate, ostensibly because of the cold weather, was generally spiked with gin. Fear made me extra cautious. At the time, I had been sober for three months and, as you can imagine, I needed to be alert to avoid having another slip. My hands still trembled and sweated. My body was just beginning to recover from the beating it had received from King Alcohol.

All this was happening on Christmas Eve, 1978. I felt desperate, not because of what might happen in combat—after all, it was my job, if necessary, to die serving my country—but because of my own internal war. I tried to be by myself and pray. The only company I had were the letters sent by fellow AAs in the Balvanera and Santa Cruz groups back in Buenos Aires. One of them wrote: "Remember, Augusto, that you have to say no to the first drink and keep thinking about your group."

I had no one to share my sorrow, my feelings of desolation and anxiety. I tried to be like an actor who does not give his inner feelings away. That was my situation in the presence of my superiors and the people under my command. But I always managed to find a corner where I could drop a few tears, call on my Higher Power, and repeat to myself, "I'm not going to drink. I'm not going to drink."

I also carried a precious object in my backpack—a card given to me by the Santa Cruz group with the Serenity Prayer printed on the back. My mind was so damaged from my 18 years of alcoholic drinking, that I couldn't even memorize the Serenity Prayer.

Let's go back to December 24th. From various parts of the country, people had sent us all kinds of alcohol. Christmas Eve dinner was nearing. Drinks were served in mugs, people were laughing, there was a loud, nerve-racking din which made me crazy. Some guys began to cry. I, thank God, was sober, and found that I could offer consolation to those who were depressed, even though there was a war raging inside of me that no one could see.

At midnight, when everyone raised their mugs for the holiday toast, I toasted with tea, and thought about the principle of AA, one alcoholic seeking another. It was then that I found one person in my section who had given up drinking, because, as he put it, "alcohol didn't agree with me." So we spent the whole evening talking until we got sleepy. When I woke up on the 25th, I felt so good! I was happy. I had met a challenge which I'd never believed I could meet. And that wasn't the only one. On the 27th, when we were informed that there would be no war, some of us were granted a home leave, so we could spend New Year's Eve with our loved ones. For me that represented another challenge: how could I spend New Year's Eve at home without drinking? But that New Year's, for the first time, I was able to say goodbye to the old year and welcome the new year sober.

I thank God for my fellow group members back home and all those who helped me out. I'm also indebted to my sponsor, Fanny, and to all those AAs who made it possible for this alcoholic to celebrate 22 years, eight months, and one day of recovery to this day, one day at a time.

Years later, when I was sent to fight in the Falklands war, I did what I had to do, carrying with me the Twelve Steps. At that time I also felt the presence of my Higher Power, but this time around, I had the certainty that comes to those of us who get used to living one day at a time.

*Augusto M.*
*Buenos Aires, Argentina*

## Door to Door Sobriety
July 1998

With about nine months' sobriety in AA, the Army transferred me to Germany. There was no AA group at the installation where I was stationed, and after about three months I slipped back into my old stinking thinking and began to drink again.

I drank for a few months more until I was beginning to get into trouble with the Army, and my family life was in shambles. Out of desperation I went to see a local physician in the health clinic. I told the doctor that I was an alcoholic and the only way I'd ever been able to stay sober was in Alcoholics Anonymous. I wondered if he had any patients who needed AA. He said, "I have a bunch of them, and if you'll come back tomorrow, I'll give you a list." I went back the next day and the list he handed me filled a page.

I went door-to-door like a salesman, and to my surprise this technique worked. The first person on the list was a warrant officer who was about to be discharged because of his alcoholism. His wife, who was a registered nurse, answered the door. I explained who I was and why I was there. She said, "Come on in, 'It' is in the bedroom." Her husband was in a fetal position on his bed and the room was completely dark. As I entered, he said, "Close the door before they get me." He was suffering from severe DTs, and his wife and I gave him a small amount of alcohol to taper him off.

He and I, along with the aid of the doctor, got an AA group started, and when I left Germany we had about 15 regular members. I'm proud to say that my first Twelfth Step call was successful. The warrant officer retired from the Army with an illustrious career. I've had the privilege of making hundreds of Twelfth Step calls since then, and many of the people I went to see didn't find sobriety, but I always left with a prayer for the suffering alcoholic and thanks to my God for my own sobriety.

*John S.*
*York, Alabama*

## Around the World
*(From: Carrying the Message)*
October 1965

**B**elieve me, the world is not such a large place when you think of all the known and unknown AA folk around. I have met them in the most unusual and peculiar places.

Last trip at Tohohama I was ashore at an Army-Navy PX, and when I was paying a check at the cashier's desk my plastic card with the Serenity Prayer and Twelve Steps on it fell out onto the desk. The chap alongside me stared at it, tapped me on the shoulder and asked if he could see the card more closely.

I handed it to him and asked if he knew what it was. Believe it or not he did. He was a Japanese cab driver who had had a lot of trouble with the sake and had been helped by a seaman who had missed his ship and was ashore for a while.

He invited me to meet some friends of his later that evening and gave me the address and directions to meet at 7:30. I went, and what a surprise! When I got there, it was the Japanese Torako Buso or Turkish bath house. My friend was waiting for me and took me inside. There in the large community bath we held an AA meeting—12 AAs.

Words could never tell the story. What is more important is the fact that AA reaches everywhere and can be held any place.

*W. G.*

*Hong Kong, China*

## A Postscript From the Sergeant
October 2005

This is a postscript to an experience I had last year in Iraq. After a couple of months with no contact with the rest of the world (I was on deployment in Al Asad, Iraq), I wrote to Grapevine and received a note from the office thanking me for my story and saying that if it was printed, I'd receive a copy of the issue. I figured that was that; I had tried to carry the message.

That night I had a drunk dream. As I usually do with these dreams, I struggled with the "after feelings." I was still wound pretty tight (I still am!), so I decided I needed to get into action again.

A day or so later, I bumped into the chaplain. I asked him if there were any AA meetings where we were in Iraq and he said, "I've heard of some elsewhere in Iraq. Why? Are you struggling?"

"No, sir," I said. "It's no longer about the drink for me. It's about carrying the message—and spirituality."

He lit up. "What faith are you?" he asked. I thought, Oh, great. How do I, as a recovering alcoholic, explain my idea of religion and spirituality to a chaplain? I told him briefly about my spiritual journey. For me, this is a "process" and not an "event" and AA is where I first became aware of it. Then I asked him to send any alcoholics he might meet in my direction. I continued on my way, somewhat discouraged.

Two or three weeks later, I was resting in the dayroom when one of my soldiers said, "Sergeant, there's a female at the door for you."

"Yeah, right," I said, "and I bet she's gorgeous, too."

"No, really, there is!" he replied.

Sure as there is a sun, there she was. She tentatively asked, "Is your name Michael?" When I said yes, her next question was even more tentative. "Are you ... a friend of Bill W.?" Immediately, I led her outside so we could visit privately.

Of course, the guys were all giving me the thumbs-up, hooting and winking and all. I just shook my head and tried to convey that it wasn't anything like that. Once outside, Linda said, "My sister told me you were here and that I should come find you. She lives in California and has been in AA seven years."

"I don't know anyone who lives in California."

Linda said, "She was reading some AA literature, something called 'the grapevine' or something." So that's how I found out my story had been published! We continued to have an incredible conversation. It pretty much turned into a meeting right there.

Linda and I met the following weekend and had a First Step meeting. It was a miracle to me. We continued to bump into each other at the chow hall, and we talked about the Steps and AA. She went on leave back to the States to see her boys, and I got orders to leave Iraq. That was the last I saw of her. I gave the chaplain my copy of the Big Book, some Grapevines, and other AA literature. (He had asked if I could start a meeting, but I had orders to leave.)

That was at the end of October. Since then, I've been back to the States (Colorado, Virginia, Iowa, Florida, South Carolina). Friends have suggested that I should write to Grapevine and relay the rest of the story. I'm sending this to you from Camp Eagle in South Korea. What a trip!

So the journey continues, one day at a time.

*Michael W.*
*Korea*

## No Matter How Far Away a Meeting May Be, It's Always Somebody's Home Group
October 1996

I n the spring of 1980 I was two years sober and a member of the U.S. Navy when my ship pulled into the African port of Mombasa, Kenya. We'd last been in port nearly two months before, in Singapore. In the meantime, our ship had participated in the failed attempt to rescue the hostages taken from the U.S. Embassy in Teheran, Iran.

To say morale was low by the time we pulled into port would be an understatement. Even among our small contingent of AA members things weren't going too well. Three of us were AA members before, after and during the whole cruise. For some time we'd held meetings twice a week in the ship's chapel, for us and anyone else who wanted to attend. We went through plenty of newcomers during the cruise; they'd join us after we left on liberty port and leave us as we entered another, only to get in enough trouble and lose enough money to want to join us as we left port again!

During this long period at sea I stopped going to the meetings regularly. I guess I had some rationale for it. What it came down to was that the other two guys weren't doing it my way! (I know now I didn't have a way!) I was pretty cocky about my sobriety and felt certain everyone else was impressed with me too. Hearing the other two guys say the same things twice a week became a bore. And these newcomers just weren't getting it or they'd stay sober longer. So I decided to wait to go to a meeting in the next port.

Mombasa was that port and, using the international directory, I determined the closest meeting would be the following evening in Nairobi, 300 miles away. I bought tickets for the trip, grabbed a shipmate who I thought would be impressed by the warm welcome I'd receive in Kenya's capital, and boarded the mini-bus the next morning.

This was no superhighway, so the going was slow enough to get us there just at twilight. As we got closer to Nairobi, I saw many tribesmen walking in large groups toward the city. It never dawned on me that I saw hardly anyone walking in the other direction. This was all quaint and something I'd get to tell my friends in the States, as they breathlessly listened to my adventures as a world-traveling AA.

On arriving in Nairobi, I called the home of the gentleman whose name was in the directory. I proudly told him I was an American sailor, in town for a few days and looking for directions to his meeting that night. I was certain these folks would want to listen to me as well but instead I was told by this polite Brit that the meeting had been canceled since the Pope happened to be visiting the next day and the city's streets were pretty much shut down. The town was overcrowded with people in for the visit and all the AAs had made other plans. A little chagrined but undaunted, I asked for directions to another meeting. There was no other meeting, I was told, but in a couple of days there would be one.

Somewhere deep inside me came a feeling I'd only known in sobriety a few times before. It was the feeling I'd so often squelched by getting loaded. The feeling was that of losing control of the situation as I had planned it. The gentleman on the other end of the line was responding to the nonchalance I was trying to convey. He had no way of knowing how scared and lonely I was until I said, "You know, Singapore was my last meeting and that was more than 50 days ago. Things have been pretty rough out there and I can really use a meeting. Is there anything you can do for me?"

Without hesitation the man said he'd call some folks over to his house and see if we couldn't have a meeting there. So we got a cab and drove off to parts unknown. During the drive, rain on the scale of a monsoon burst from the sky and we had to stop to let that pass. Roads were blocked off in anticipation of the Pope the next day. It took 30 minutes to get to the house.

Seven people were there. Seven AA members had left their homes and their plans for the evening because another AA had reached out and asked for help. These folks encountered the same rain as me, navigated the same road closures, and got there in order not to see a world traveler, but to help a drunk who needed help. I don't remember a single thing that was said at that meeting. I just remember the hands that reached out to me. (I do remember the dramatic painting of a charging elephant over the fireplace—probably the only feature which distinguished this meeting from any other I've gone to.)

When I got back to the ship, I reinvested myself in the shipboard meetings and two months later, upon return to homeport and then civilian life, threw myself into AA. Sixteen years later, I go to two or more meetings a week, work with others, and reach out to travelers whenever they make themselves known.

There's really nothing new being said at meetings, but I try to go on "the give" rather than on "the take" and that makes the content of the sharing unimportant. What's important is that people are sharing at all—that they are there asking for help. It's my job to make sure the hand of AA is there for them.

I still stifle my growth by hiding behind the image I want everyone to have of me, and I grow whenever I get honest about that. These days I spend a lot more time being myself. I have a lot more experience in that area, and I have the AAs in Nairobi to thank for showing me what people will do when I ask for help. AA is free, it's worldwide, and it works.

No matter how far away a meeting may be—across town or across the globe—it's always somebody's home group.

*Mark L.*
*Austin, Texas*

## Is That You Again?
*(Excerpt)*
October 1994

W hen I was a young soldier in the Canadian Armed Forces during World War II, I had no problem with alcohol. But in the postwar years my drinking progressed. I had stayed in the Army and I soon began to be disciplined for my conduct while under the influence. The military told me I was a "sloppy" drinker, which I now understand to mean I was sloppy in dress, sloppy with time, sloppy with other people's money. Eventually they called me an alcoholic. I was introduced to AA by an Army commanding officer on July 15, 1956 and have been sober ever since.

AA helped correct my bad habits, and with nine years' sobriety I was posted to Camp Rafah in Egypt, for a one-year tour of duty with the United Nations. I expected to be a "Loner" over there so I took a lot of AA literature with me. But somehow on the airplane, my sober thinking began to evaporate. The slogan "Just for Today" completely left me and was replaced by the thought that maybe I had wasted nine years in AA—maybe I wasn't an alcoholic after all. I was going 4,000 miles away from home, and if I drank again, nobody would know. This thinking went on for the duration of the 17-hour flight, and by the time I landed in the Gaza Strip, I could almost taste the alcohol. Fortunately for me, when the door of the aircraft opened after my long flight, there were two alcoholics waiting for me.

Charlie and Lynn, although drinking at the time, had been instructed by the commanding officer in Egypt to organize an AA group at Camp Rafah. The officer, faced with a serious drinking problem among the personnel, had written a padre back in Ontario for AA literature, and the padre had sent, along with the literature, the names of two known alcoholics in Egypt. These were Charlie and Lynn, who now informed me I was the fourth member of their little AA group.

Our meeting place was an old camel shed that had originally been used by the British Army during the First World War. Charlie and Lynn had cleaned it up and supplied it with white linen tablecloths and china cups and saucers. This made for quite a contrast! Meanwhile, the military police were in the habit of firing light shotgun pellets to disperse wild dog packs from the camp, and every so often the pellets would spatter against the tin siding of our shed. Many a newcomer dodged for cover under our linen-covered tables.

The meetings provided not only sobriety, but strong lessons in tolerance and compassion. Some of our members were not exactly pleased about being ordered to attend AA meetings and needed a lot of encouragement. Not everyone stayed sober, but by the time I left we had 28 members.

We had a lot of help and support from others. The group was encouraged by the commanding officers, and we were often visited by both Catholic and Protestant padres, which added to our spiritual well-being. The General Service Office in New York sent us tapes and materials, and the tapes were not only used privately, but were a good source of topics during the meetings. New York also provided us with contacts who were Loners in the Middle East, and we were able to reach a few of them.

Today, there are numerous meetings and conferences here at home. That wasn't the case in the Middle East in the mid-60s. Furthermore, alcohol was readily available to any guest in a hotel. When you called room service for a soft drink, a complete rolling bar would be delivered to your room. Look out! So, like soldiers everywhere, we AAs learned to depend on each other to survive. When we toured the Holy Land and the Old World, we always traveled in pairs and returned to the safety of camp if there was the slightest temptation to drink.

The experiences of that year in the Middle East are the sort that only happen once in a lifetime, and I'm grateful to have been a part of it. Today life goes on for me in the AA program. I'm glad to say that

Irene, my wife of 49 years, my five sons, four daughters-in-law, and 17 grandchildren all still tolerate me.

When Irene and I were first married, she'd give me a peck on the cheek when I left for work in the morning, call me "Lovey," and wish me a good day. When my drinking became a major problem, "Have a good day" changed to "I hope you drop dead." Now when I leave home, Irene says: "Have you got your teeth, your hearing aid, and your glasses? Did you take your pills today?" And when I return home, her first words are, "Is that you again?"

*Pat B.*
*Oakville, Ontario*

CHAPTER SIX

# Women Serving Their Country

Women soldiers share their experiences about
getting and staying sober

---

**T**he role of women in the military has evolved significantly since World War II—and the stories in Grapevine reflect this. Consider that since the 1990s, women have been able to serve in combat zones. The very nature of military service (ships at sea, remote postings, limited communications), which can inadvertently isolate AAs from the Fellowship, has always posed challenges for alcoholics trying to get and stay sober. The women in this chapter show us how it's done.

Patty S. of Romeoville, Illinois writes in her story, "My Guardian Angel," that she joined the Army in 1986 to escape her alcoholism, but found that it followed her wherever she went. While stationed in Germany soon after the fall of the Berlin Wall, a soldier named Angel took her to her first AA meeting. Patty drank again, but kept trying. Indeed, in 2017, when her story was published, Patty had 26 years of sobriety. She spent years trying to find Angel to thank him, but no luck. Then finally one day her efforts paid off. "Miracles do happen in this program all the time," she writes.

In a story from 2005, "Desert Oasis," Heather C. arrived in Iraq as a member of the armed forces and a member of AA. She writes that there were no AA groups at "my camp." So she started making Twelfth Step calls referred to her by the base chaplain. With these new recruits, she started an AA group. Where did Heather get these ideas? It's what the Big Book "told me to do," she writes.

And in the article "Woman Adrift," Carolyn I. of La Mesa, California writes that she had 16 months of sobriety when she entered the

*Navy. She was assigned to a U.S. destroyer and was sent to East Asia and then the Persian Gulf. "Sobriety in Alcoholics Anonymous gave me the freedom to go anywhere and do anything I wanted to do," she writes.*

## Woman Adrift
May 2005

I joined the Navy in September 1983, from my hometown of Costa Mesa, California. I had been sober for about 16 months. You see, I had wanted to join the Navy for several years, but couldn't imagine going through boot camp without a drink. Sobriety in Alcoholics Anonymous gave me the freedom to go anywhere and do anything I wanted to do.

I did boot camp in Orlando, Florida, and received specialized training in Great Lakes, Illinois. Then I was sent to a ship, the USS Acadia AD-42, a destroyer tender. I was assigned to the ship just as the Navy was beginning to allow women to be stationed aboard. I was one of about 40 women out of a crew of some 1500 sailors. When I left some three years later, there were about 400 women on board. The time in boot camp and Navy school made it easy to stay sober as there wasn't much booze, if any, around. But onboard ship, at least in port, it seemed that alcohol played a major role in many sailors' lives.

I was very fortunate there were other recovering alcoholics. We sought each other out and had meetings onboard ship, and even though I was the only female, this group became my support and I was theirs. During my time onboard, I was deployed on two Western Pacific cruises. Between the first and second deployment, I was married, which made leaving again even harder.

The times at sea would become lonely, even with the support of my shipmates in recovery. Mail calls were few and far between. If I received a letter from home, I would carry it around for days in my pocket, reading it again and again. I never strayed far from my Big Book or "Twelve and Twelve." The words of those who had gone before me gave me great comfort and hope. I would often write out a phrase from the Big Book like "we pause, when agitated or doubtful, and ask for the right thought or direction." I would tape it to the ceiling of my rack and read it before the lights went out at night and again when they went on in the morning. The reminder that God was with me even way out in the middle of the ocean encouraged me. In the "Twelve and Twelve" in Step Three, it talks about how critical being dependent on a Higher Power is. It gives examples of those in the services during WW II. It says that often the soldiers fared better than those in recovery at home because they were forced to draw strength from their Higher Power.

I also stayed in contact with the ship's chaplain so that he knew I was available to help others if he saw the need arise. Getting out of myself was often a way to forget about my troubles and loneliness. I went to church services too—any way that I could find to connect with God was helpful.

When my ship hit port in such places as the Philippines, Japan, Hong Kong or Korea, I searched out meetings while a lot of my shipmates hit the bars. I also traveled into the Persian Gulf to repair the USS Start that was hit by a stray Iraqi missile, in which 30 sailors lost their lives. Traveling through the Straits of Hormuz was scary. We were the first ship with women onboard to enter the Gulf. Our unarmed ship was flanked by destroyers, and we remained at general quarters for most of the day. The tension that prevailed was constant for the entire time in the Gulf, as we spent several weeks there in Bahrain. Again, I drew on my Higher Power for courage and peace of mind through prayer, meditation and reading my books. Fortunately, there were about eight or 10 local sober people in Bahrain who hung together and had meetings of Alcoholics Anonymous daily. I feel so fortunate to have met brothers and sisters in sobriety all over the world. What a joy! And just like here at home, I was glad to socialize with these folks outside the meetings too. I'm sure that as a result, I got to do and see much more than most of my other shipmates. I feel so blessed to have these experiences in sobriety, and I will never forget hearing the "language of the heart" in so many places around the world.

I finished my enlistment in September 1987 still sober, and have remained sober ever since. I'm sure that as with those who went before me, my sobriety was strengthened by my military experience. So, to my fellow soldiers, sailors, airmen, marines and all others way from home, keep the faith and trust in your Higher Power for courage and strength. God's grace is with us for the asking and each day sober is a miraculous gift from God.

*Carolyn I.*
*La Mesa, California*

## Desert Oasis
May 2005

My name is Heather and I am an alcoholic currently serving in Iraq. I was dismayed to read in a recent Grapevine that another member of the armed forces was having to go it alone. When I first arrived here, there was no AA group at my camp. I felt alone, and I was scared that after two years of seeing what happens to people who don't make meetings, I wasn't making meetings. However, "Bill's Story" in the Big Book gives a very clear example of what to do when work with other alcoholics is needed; it also gives further instructions in the chapter "Working With Others."

I went to both my chaplain and the mental health specialist. It took a few months, but eventually I found another alcoholic. At that point we put up a couple of signs with a meeting time. The important thing was that I didn't sit and wait for someone to find me. I went out and did what the Big Book told me to do. My sobriety and my sanity were worth going to any lengths.

Our group is now up to three people. Because of our schedules we're only able to meet once a week. However, I supplement meetings with Grapevine, the Loners-Internationalists Meeting and online meetings. I am also happy that I've had the opportunity to do two

Twelfth Step calls with personnel here at the camp. Both were referrals from the chaplain.

Many of us have come to take the existence of a meeting for granted. The experience of having to search out other alcoholics in a place where AA doesn't exist points out how God worked through the oldtimers. It also gives me a new appreciation for the Traditions. I thank God every day for my fellow alcoholics here in Iraq.

*Heather C.*
*Iraq*

## Making Her Meeting
September 2010

t was hot, sweaty summertime and I was temporarily assigned to the Middle East. I'd been sober for six months. I tried to take care of myself by eating well, drinking plenty of water, running when the temperature was not over 100º F. and even volunteering at the post library to stay out of trouble. At my last duty station, my sponsor and I had worked through the Steps as far as we could, given the circumstances. A few good men had made a few good suggestions about finding meetings: check with the senior enlisted advisor, the chief nurse and the chaplain. The chaplain said that "recovering alcoholics used to meet at the base occasionally, but none have lately, which is to be expected when troops rotate so often." Relieved, I said, "Mind if I 'meet' with myself?"

I prayed our prayers, read the readings, studied a story or two from the Big Book and went back to my room. One night, after about 20 minutes, two men joined me. One was originally from the local area, and the other was a diplomat with the whitest shirt and shiniest loafers I had ever seen. Almost out of breath, they apologized for being late. They had been delayed while going through security measures at the gate. Perhaps my guardian angel chaplain told them about my erstwhile meeting of one. We opened with the same prayers and readings, which were comforting, and then one of the fellows began sharing about his daughter's boyfriend. I knew I was right at home.

Over the summer, the meeting grew to twos and threes, and sometimes more. One night an older gent with sobriety in the double-digits came in. We hugged. Overseas for the first time, he was filled with gratitude. I, on the other hand, had been away from home for as long as I could remember, but only sober for less than a year. We supported each other using the language of the heart.

One day there was a terrible vehicle accident. Our military unit lost several people on the road to the airport. We all took it very hard. Having been next to some of those people that very morning, we were faced with our own mortality and how fragile life can be. Within a day or so, I found myself sitting in the meeting. Still devastated, I shared how shaken I was feeling. I also told them that I couldn't find the strength and confidence to send the troops back on that road even though I knew the mission called for it and extensive safety checks had been completed.

My AA friend said something that I must have heard many times before. He said, "Some people say our program boils down to three things. Number two is clean house; number three is help others. But number one might be especially helpful: trust God." I smile now while writing these words. But at that time, I thought, Sure, old man, thanks for caring and thanks for sharing but ... yeah, but .... Honestly, I had no answer for that one (as if it were a question). Trust God.

I am pretty sure he continued to share, though I have no clue what he might have said. Slowly, gradually, I looked up from the floor with a little relief. He smiled and I smiled back. Maybe he winked. That's the way I want to remember it. We went for a burger just so I could keep that good feeling for as long as possible. His words took me back on that road and back home on the airplane and a long way since.

Eventually we had to go our separate ways, that night and in life. For a little while, I thought about trying to find him. But it was such a great lesson in anonymity. Our names, faces and identities did not matter at all. What did matter was that one alcoholic was sharing with another.

*Dawn G.*
*Kenosha, Wisconsin*

# Walking the Walk
October 2017

started drinking when I was 14. I loved it. Alcohol helped me to feel like I could do anything. The rules didn't apply to me when I was drunk. Back then I could only drink on the weekends and alcohol was difficult to obtain.

As I got older, alcohol was much easier to come across and my drinking became an every-other-day thing. Alcohol was still fun but soon I was left feeling like something was missing. I felt as though I needed to do more with my life. So I enlisted in the Marine Corps.

I couldn't drink at boot camp. After those 13 weeks, I got drunk twice on boot-leave. I went on to Marine Combat Training, where alcohol wasn't available, then to Military Occupational Specialties (MOS) school. I knew from my past experience with alcohol that when I drank, I got very drunk. I managed to stay sober and alone that first weekend at MOS school. The next weekend I went out and got drunk and made a lot of "friends."

I picked Okinawa as a duty station because I had heard that people out there liked to drink as I liked to drink. Sure enough, I arrived in Okinawa to a company that called themselves "Alphaholics." Everyone drank like me, or so I thought. My drinking usually occupied the whole weekend, Friday through Sunday. Then it quickly progressed to Thursday through Sunday. Before long I was on daily maintenance.

I almost got kicked off of a deployment for making trouble with a company PT. I let down a lot of people, made bad decisions. Yet I continued to do the same thing over and over again.

Deployment came and for the first month, I detoxed. It was awful. I remember how insane I felt, the shakes, dehydration. But then I started to feel better.

People were nice to me. They told me how much better a human I was when I was sober. I had sworn off alcohol, I was done forever.

But when I got back from deployment, there was a six-pack waiting in the fridge for me at the barracks. People were drinking all around me. Who was I not to join in? I got drunk and stayed drunk for the next four months. I tried all I could to stop, but all I could do was string together two days at most.

God has a way of working things out. One night, at 3 A.M., I was drinking a beer alone. I was full of pity, self-hate and remorse. I had that loneliness that all alcoholics know. All of a sudden I had the thought that there had to be a better way of living than this.

With the help of a friend (also a godsend), I put myself into an outpatient program, courtesy of the Corps. That was September 2012. My intention was to learn how to "control" my drinking. They sent me to AA and by God's grace, I did what I was told. It's the best thing that ever happened to me. I got a Big Book, got a sponsor and started doing the Steps. I haven't had to take a drink since then.

As a newly sober member of AA, just 21 years old and in the Marine Corps, I was sent off to Thailand. I had four months of sobriety at the time and was terrified that I would get drunk. All I had was my Big Book, my "Twelve and Twelve" and some issues of Grapevine. And God.

Every night, my platoon was getting drunk, including my higher-ups. I felt like I wanted to die and wondered why God put me in a situation like that. I prayed a lot, read the literature whenever I could and, if not for Grapevine, my "meeting away from a meeting," I would be drunk today. Grapevine stories kept me going when I was unable to attend an AA meeting in person.

By God's grace, I wanted to stay sober more than I wanted to drink. Today, I'm happily sober. If you're new to AA and in the military with no support for your sobriety, you will always have God and the literature. I now look back at Thailand as the trip that is the foundation of my sobriety. I haven't had any circumstances that have been or will be as rough as it was staying sober with four months of sobriety in Thailand. God can get you through too.

*Jen S.*
*San Antonio, Texas*

## Navy Lady

*(From: Dear Grapevine)*
July 1979

I recently celebrated my first anniversary of sobriety in AA. I also celebrated my 21st birthday. At first, it was impossible for anyone to tell me I had a drinking problem. I was too young; I had too much willpower. Besides, how many females are alcoholics? I always felt that the females who were alcoholics weren't ladies.

I was forced into AA under threat of a bad-conduct discharge from the Navy. At that point, I really didn't care. My personnel jacket was thick enough to make a book, very little of it saying anything good. Such entries as "Frequently comes to duty drunk," "Drinks on duty," and "Loses control of herself when she drinks," dotted my record from boot camp days.

After my initial resentments about anyone or anything to do with AA, I began to learn in spite of myself. At every meeting, I've learned something new. I know that it is only through the grace of God, and with the help of AA, that I've stayed sober. And sobriety is the best thing that ever happened to me.

*S. R.*
*Zion, Illinois*

## Heart to Heart

August 2001

During the summer of 1995, I was transferred from Washington, D.C. (where AA meetings are abundant) to the Moslem country of Bahrain, a small island 15 miles off the eastern coast of Saudi Arabia. As a U.S. Navy sailor with 10 months of sobriety, my main concern was how I'd maintain my AA program. After all, the stereotypical thinking goes, the Moslems don't drink, so I wondered if AA would be nonexistent except for meetings on the base. I was newly sober, recovering from a three-year relapse after 16 years of continuous sobriety. But I knew that in any random group of people, one in 10 has a drinking problem, and I strongly suspected that Bahrainis were no different. Perhaps more of them hid their problem, since the stigma of alcoholism in Moslem countries was a lot worse—still, there must be an AA meeting somewhere in Bahrain. And I thought nothing was going to stand in the way of my sobriety. I had to learn that I could stand in the way of my sobriety.

My first impression of Bahrain that hot and humid night at Bahrain International Airport was a feeling of calm mixed with mystery and adventure. At four in the morning, asleep in my hotel room, I was awakened by the beckoning sound of the Grand Mosque's Call to Prayer (my room faced that beautiful mosque by the sea), and that prayer call started my intrigue with this island. Soon, the Call to Prayer, heard five times a day—at roughly sunrise, midday, mid-afternoon, sunset, and evening—focused me on my spiritual condition, moving my attention inward. It became a gentle reminder to check in on myself and take inventory, similar to my response to the church bells ringing in the villages and cities of Europe when I was stationed there. It was another tool in my AA toolbox.

I'd learned from my relapse that "it works if you work it, and it won't if you don't." Also, I knew from my relapse that the number one cause of my relapse was not going to meetings. Nevertheless, I was in Bahrain almost three weeks before I checked out the meeting situation. I rationalized that working every day for 14 hours left no time for anything but an evening jog by the sea, a quick supper and sleep. Sooner or later, I reasoned, I'd get to AA, but not right then. I was too busy.

Soon, however, my commander asked me if I was going to AA meetings and motivated me to go to the base drug/alcohol program advisor, who promptly handed me a schedule of AA meetings in Bahrain. There was one every night, some at a church, others at a hospital, one in an AA member's home, all English-speaking. My rationalizations had blinded me to the fact that I was falling into the old pattern—that of drifting away from AA.

I went to a meeting that Monday night at a church and then on Thursday night at the American Mission Hospital. At last, I came back into the calm, reassuring, good feeling of an AA meeting. Instantly, I felt connected again, heart to heart. These two meetings became my steady diet of strength, hope and fellowship. I made a promise to myself to attend meetings regularly. I picked certain nights for meetings and resolved that nothing short of war (literally, my having to report to a battle station) would prevent me from going. I kept my promise and my integrity deepened.

And so what began as an intrigue with this island evolved into a love affair with sober life in Bahrain. I developed a strong attraction to the AA Fellowship here. Because of our small meetings (four to 10 people), we always have an opportunity to share. We usually see the same faces, so our meetings offer a special closeness not found in bigger meetings.

Now, as I depart Bahrain in a few weeks, I'm glad because I do want to return home. But I'm also sad. (It's the familiar condition of mixed emotions. Don't these ever stop appearing?)

Bahrain is where I grew stronger, made spiritual progress and began to learn the meaning of a daily reprieve. Here is where my AA program took shape, and took on discipline and commitment to daily maintenance. The door was open; it was up to me to enter. Life is what I make it.

*Barbara T.*
*Manama, Bahrain*

## My Guardian Angel
October 2017

I was a 22-year-old female soldier in 1989, living in southern Bavaria. The Berlin Wall had just come down, and it was a crazy time mixed with lots of beerfests and blackouts for me. I had joined the Army in 1986 to escape my alcoholism, but it followed me wherever I went. I was unable to make rank because I was always blacking out and getting into fights and causing trouble. I kept getting knocked off the promotion list.

I always hung out with people who drank as much as me so I didn't feel like such a wreck. One of my friends was sent to alcohol counseling sessions because she had been getting into trouble as well. Although I was not mandated, I went with her one time because I knew I was a mess and I was getting really tired of feeling like such a loser.

The counseling was in Munich, Germany, and we had to ride a shuttle bus an hour each way to get there. I would go in with her and listen. I didn't hear much in the session because I was too busy checking out one of the guys in the group. He wore an Army uniform with a name tag that read "Angel." I thought it was a cool name and I was attracted to him because he seemed smart and was good-looking. I can't remember what I said in the session, but I must have made quite an impression because Angel came up to me after the meeting. He said he wanted to take me somewhere, and asked if I was free that night. I was so excited. I thought I was being asked out on a date. Little did I know he would bring me to my very first AA meeting.

He drove an hour to pick me up, and then an hour back to Munich where the meeting was. There were only two other people at the meeting. They were Germans who spoke broken English, but they gave me a copy of the Twelve Steps to read. I read them for the first time and could not believe what I saw. It was like they were written for me. The people there somehow knew how my life was unmanageable and out of control. They knew I needed help and how desperate and alone I was. I felt a sense of belonging for the first time in my life. I think cried the entire meeting.

After the meeting, I waited for Angel to make a move on me. I was not used to men who didn't have a hidden agenda. In my world, everyone had an ulterior motive. Instead, he took me back to his barracks and introduced me to a couple of his friends who were also sober—and young.

They told me life did not have to be boring just because I didn't drink anymore. They handed me a copy of the Big Book and explained a little about the program. I was in a fog so I don't remember much more than that. He drove me all the way home, and during the hour he talked to me about sobriety. He was a perfect gentleman, and I never saw him again.

I ended up going into inpatient treatment at the Army hospital in Nuremberg. After I got out, I was shipped back to the United States. I am guessing the Army felt I could not make it through another Octoberfest without falling off the wagon.

I was sent to Kelly Air Force Base in San Antonio, Texas. Soon I decided since I'd had a fresh start, I didn't need to go to AA meetings. After all, I had all the knowledge I needed to stay sober on my own. But as soon as Desert Storm began, I found an excuse to drink again. Within two weeks I was miserable and drunk. It was not long before there were two strangers (and a dog) living in my apartment with me.

About that time, the Army was asking for volunteers to go to the Middle East where the fighting was taking place. I was so depressed that I was the first to volunteer because the idea of being shot in battle sounded better than having to try and sober up again.

Then one day in November of 1990, I came out of a blackout sitting on the floor, barricaded in my room, holding a knife. I was at the jumping off place. I was not able to enjoy alcohol anymore because I knew I had a problem I could not solve on my own. I had a head full of AA and it had ruined my drinking. I went over to my closet and found my Big Book and closed my eyes. I very defiantly asked God to prove his existence to me. I opened the book to a page and saw this passage:

"If you are as seriously alcoholic as we were, we believe there is no middle-of-the-road solution. We were in a position where life was becoming impossible, and if we had passed into the region from which there is no return through human aid, we had but two alternatives: One was to go on to the bitter end, blotting out the consciousness of our intolerable situation as best we could; and the other, to accept spiritual help."

There was my answer. I went back to Alcoholics Anonymous and found a sponsor right away. I decided to do whatever they asked of me. I gradually learned how to live life on life's terms and I learned acceptance. I cleaned ashtrays and earned my chair at the meetings.

I got out of the Army in 1992 and moved back to my hometown. I became a police officer, got married and had three children. I have been very successful in my career and have had a happy, sober and fulfilling life.

I've often wondered if my first meeting was real. It's still hard to believe there actually was someone wearing a name tag that read "Angel" out there who guided me to my first meeting. It seems that I dreamed the whole thing in a blackout. After a few years, I began to search online for people named Angel and for more than 20 years, I had no luck.

This past year, I celebrated 26 years of sobriety. In the last few years, I did not like running into people I had arrested and dealt with in my profession, and I began using that as an excuse to stay away from the program. But I recently found out about a group of police officers who have a regular AA meeting nearby, so I no longer have an excuse not to attend.

One night, before the police officer meeting, I was scrolling through my phone when a message popped up. It was someone accepting my friend request. I looked, and it was someone named Angel. I sent him back a message and asked if he had been in the Army, stationed in Munich, Germany in 1989. He said that he had! It was indeed my real-life guardian angel, and after a little bit of chatting back and forth, he remembered me too! I had not dreamed it up after all. My Higher Power actually sent someone with a name tag from heaven so I could not miss him.

Angel told me his father was in AA for 40 years. He said he is no longer attending meetings, but lives a good life and was happy to know that he made a difference in mine. I believe my Higher Power knew I was really sick and not capable of listening unless he sent a good-looking guy my way and placed a name tag on him!

I now go to meetings regularly and I stay in touch with Angel. I will be forever grateful for my old friend. Miracles do happen in this program all the time. That's how this program works.

*Patty S.*
*Romeoville, Illinois*

CHAPTER SEVEN

# Coming Home

### Experience, strength and hope from sober veterans

---

**F**or veterans, war often comes home with them. In this chapter, veterans of World War II, Korea, Vietnam and the Middle East share their struggles and how they used the AA program to get sober, stay sober, or get sober again.

In the story "Incoming!" by Eric C. of Traverse City, Michigan, a Marine who fought during Operation Desert Storm finds himself in Somalia during a civil war. The AA meeting he and his fellow soldiers hold gets broken up by sniper fire—more than once. "It was our group's little joke that we closed our meetings "in the usual manner,'" Eric writes, "by all shouting 'Incoming!'" At the time veteran Eric wrote this Grapevine story, he had 33 years sober.

In "Eternal Point," member Jerry E. of Beavercreek, Ohio has one of his worst hangovers while "smack in the middle of Viet Cong country" and threatens "to kill my company commander." Returning home, he gets sober, but memories of Vietnam drive him "to my knees," he recalls. He starts an AA meeting for vets like him, hoping to help those struggling with their wartime experiences. "There are no excuses to drink today," he writes, then adds, "sure as heck not Vietnam stuff."

Member Bill G. of Albany, New York writes in "Me Against the World" that he had "13 shots of vodka" the day before entering his local VA hospital for alcoholic hepatitis. On the detox-acute psychiatric ward for a month, he saw veterans of World War II, Korea and Vietnam. Today, he puts his yearly anniversary medallions next to his Silver Star, Bronze Star and two Purple Hearts.

## Me Against the World
January 1997

I took my last 13 shots of vodka on the day before I entered my local VA hospital for alcoholic hepatitis due to not eating enough while drinking. Once my liver was fixed up, I figured I'd take better care of myself and eat a little (while drinking).

Well, they checked me in, and I weighed 117 pounds on a 5'11" frame. The doctor complimented me on my fine teeth. I joked and hammed it up for the nurses, trying to show how nonchalant I was. Inside, I was terrified. I knew they didn't serve alcohol in the VA.

After spending a day on a medical-surgical floor, I was indignant when the doctor said, "Send him up to the psychiatric floor. Let them detox him." My Silver Star, Bronze Star, and two Purple Hearts didn't seem to impress them much as they took me upstairs to the 10th floor. You see, I'd always thought of myself as a little weird, but not crazy. Besides, wasn't I a hero, a combat veteran? Sure, I'd drunk a little more than I should have, but I was entitled. The nightmares, the night sweats, the startle reflex at any loud noise—that's why I drank. Couldn't they see that an ungrateful country which chose to ignore me and other Vietnam vets was responsible for my excess drinking? Surely the VA would be sympathetic, they would understand. They understood, all right!

After a month with no alcohol in the detox-acute psychiatric ward, I saw other vets—vets from World War II, Korea, and Vietnam. I noticed there were two types of vets up there. Those who were discharged from the hospital sober, and in a week or two returned to be readmitted drunk, and those who were discharged from the hospital, period. There was a vet with "wet brain," another going through DTs, and still another screaming all night in the isolation room for his mother to hold him. That was me. The fact that she died three months after my return from Vietnam was a reason to drink. It was me, alone, against a loused-up world. Sound familiar?

After spending 89 days on the psychiatric ward, I was discharged from the hospital. I remember the nurse saying, "Your best chance of staying sober is after your first hospitalization for alcoholism." The only thing was, I didn't think I was an alcoholic. I'd gotten 100 percent on the questionnaire about my drinking habits: yes, I drank alone; yes, I drank in the morning; yes, I drank every day for over five years. But I still had a house, money in the bank, and my dog. I didn't need to learn how to feed myself like they were teaching the guys up on the ward. I had a master's degree in English literature and had taught for eight years. OK, I was on a temporary medical leave of absence. Sure, my wife had left me, but I divorced her. The doctors said I was suffering from an anxiety disorder and post-traumatic stress disorder from seeing too much combat. They used to call it shell shock or battle fatigue. I wasn't going to take their advice about taking my medication and attending AA meetings. AA was for skidrow deadbeats, and I was a war hero. I'd do it like I did everything in life—alone, with no help from anybody.

I got into my 11-year-old car, my hand still shaking as I put the key in the ignition. I was free. The engine turned over after three tries and off I drove. The 89 days in the psychiatric ward were worse than combat, worse than 'Nam, worse than anything I'd ever experienced. I wouldn't make the same mistake again.

I was stopped at a red light, about two blocks from the hospital, when I saw it: Papa's Bar and Grill. Suddenly, the car stalled. The car behind me began honking. I felt trapped in the car. "A drink, I need a drink." With that thought, I knew I was licked before I started. In my desperation, I asked God to take my life right then and there. I couldn't win this battle and I wasn't going back to the terror and captivity of the psychiatric ward. I didn't want to drink anymore, but seemed powerless to stop. For the first time in my life, I knew I was beaten. My will and determination were useless. "God, I quit. You heal me if you want but I quit," I said in desperation. "If you want me sober then you start this car." I looked anxiously at the bar and then to the ignition key. Shaking, I turned the key. The engine turned over instantly, I turned the corner, got home, and on my 90th day dry went to my first AA meeting.

I haven't had a drink since those 13 vodkas the day I went to the VA and that was in January 1985. Today I have friends, hope, serenity and honesty. I put my yearly anniversary medallions above my Silver Star, Bronze Star and two Purple Hearts, because they were tougher to get. Today I really feel like a hero!

*Bill G.*
*Albany, New York*

## Eternal Point
January 1997

My name is Jerry and I'm an alcoholic. I'm also a drug addict and a Vietnam vet. So, I'm lots of things besides the child of God that was made for some reason I'll never understand while I'm here on earth.

My last drink was taken on June 24, 1982. I went nearly 14 months past that date before I regularly began attending AA meetings. Prior to that, the longest I'd gone without a drink was several weeks. Those periods included some time in Vietnam where I promised myself I wouldn't drink or drug in the bush because it was too dangerous. But within a very short time, I broke that rule and drank and drugged out at a fire base smack in the middle of Viet Cong country. The next day, carrying one of the worst hangovers I've ever had, I threatened to kill my company commander. He threatened me with court martial but I got shot several days later. That took me into a year-long stay in Army hospitals. But aside from several weeks in intensive care wards, even that didn't restrain my drinking. This all happened in 1966. It took me 16 more years one day at a time to get to AA.

It seems like God, my eternal friend, has always thrown stones in front of me to walk on, through this Zen garden he or she has created for me. Oddly enough, they're always where they're supposed to be, and at the right time.

Al-Anon was one. I started Al-Anon in 1982 because my brother and dad "had a problem with alcohol." The music sounded familiar but I couldn't quite get the rhythm of the dance step. Then I wound up in AA. The music was right and once I relaxed and found, as it says in "Doctor, Alcoholic, Addict," that I "was an alcoholic of sorts," the dance steps came more naturally.

Recovering became one-day-at-a-time personal. Today, I can say that while I may not have become instantly raving drunk on drink number one, I never could tell where that first one would lead me. Alienation, depression, loneliness, self-loathing and other emotions swamped me once I started. Then came remorse, shame and guilt. And often thoughts of Vietnam.

As the "Twelve and Twelve" says in Step Four, we had millions of excuses to drink including, "because our nation had won a war or lost a peace." Even in sobriety I would cry the blues or rail at God because I wasn't the hero I wanted to be or that I'd survived when so many others with more worth had died.

Somewhere around 1987, at a workshop on healing, the leader asked us to list the things we were willing to accept responsibility for in order to heal. She warned we had to expect that with the healing would come some pain. Vietnam was one of the half-dozen things I listed. She said God would decide which would come first.

Within weeks, a guy who'd gone into basic training with me found me after 22 years. Then I ran into a Vietnam vet in AA. We went to see a popular movie about Vietnam together, and we processed our pain and reaction to the movie. I found a guy who'd been with me the day I got shot. He sent me pictures of a good friend who'd been killed after I left. I met more vets in AA. Around this time, there was a piece on national television about the pain many nurses who served in Vietnam have gone through. I owed so much to them for their care the year I was hospitalized. Those memories drove me to my knees, then to the phone to call my sponsor. He and another old-timer in the program encouraged me to start a meeting for AA vets here in Dayton.

The suggestion provoked lots of fear about being criticized by the AA community for setting ourselves apart. The people pleaser in me was frightened to take the step, but in the end I didn't do it alone. Five of us started Recovering 'Nam Vets in March 1989.

Since then, the topics have ranged from the emotional deserts some of us live in to flashbacks, post-traumatic stress disorder, survivor guilt and other Vietnam-related stuff. But it's an open AA meeting, and there have been other times when nonveterans have come and talked about whatever they needed to talk about, and we've done that because in the beginning we agreed we'd stay in the AA solution, not the alcoholic problem.

Alcoholics Anonymous is my solution today to all my problems. There are no excuses to drink today—sure as heck not Vietnam stuff. God is on eternal point for me, always out there ahead of me, walking down the path of life I'm on, knowing where all the mines and booby traps are, ready to help me over them, around them, or, more often today, through them. God is always ready to help if I stumble or trip, ready to help me recover if I screw things up. All I have to do is be willing to ask for help and let go. I'm sober, clean, alive, well and on a healing, recovering journey.

*Jerry E.*
*Beavercreek, Ohio*

## A Soldier Comes Home
January 2007

In July of 1986, I walked out of an AA meeting and drank. I drank for three months until I was found on the streets of Glendale, Arizona, with a backpack, 10 dollars in change, and a nearly empty bottle of vodka. I'll never forget that day. There was nothing left. I felt empty, hopeless and alone. I was done.

A policeman found me. I don't know his name, but I suspect he was a member of the Fellowship. Two men visited me in the drunk tank, and I recognized one from previous encounters with AA. That night, he said something I'll never forget: "John, you have a choice. You can either get sober and live, or drink and die. We don't care which. It's your choice."

That evening, I went to my second "first meeting." For two weeks I cried, babbled and moaned. One night, a lady named Myra with 32 years in AA told me to shut up and listen. In doing so, she used a couple of expletives that made me angry. But I listened and I stayed. My first year was not easy, but sometimes I wish I was still in it. All I had to do was go to meetings and then for coffee afterward.

Soon, I'll have 21 years of sobriety. The obsession to drink left me long ago, and today I concentrate on the miracles that have happened since that day I died and came back to life.

In my first year of sobriety, I went back to school to become a nurse. I belonged to the Army Reserve and lived on less than $200 a month, but there were always food and fellowship to keep me alive.

Here's one of the miracles. The first sergeant in my first school at Fort Sam Houston was a member of AA and allowed me to attend meetings. I graduated in 1987. I entered a school for licensed practical nursing a year later, and the lieutenant colonel in charge of that school had been sober in AA for more than 20 years.

Eight years later, I graduated from an accredited nursing school as a registered nurse. The night after graduation, I went to the Saturday night Broadway discussion meeting. I looked over and saw the course director sitting several seats to my right. Judy V. looked up and saw me. "There was always something about you I liked," she said.

I'll tell you about another miracle. I was called back to active duty for Operation Desert Storm and I spent nine months in Saudi Arabia and Kuwait before returning home in 1991. When we arrived at Westover Air Force Base in Massachusetts, I didn't want to get off the plane—the pilot said there was a homecoming. Back in 1970, after

Vietnam, we didn't get a warm homecoming. I had carried a rage buried so deep inside that I didn't dig it out, even for my Fourth Step.

Finally, we were ordered to leave the plane, and I stepped off to see a red carpet, 50 state flags, and a band playing for the 32 of us who had flown back. About 5,000 people filled the hangar waiting to welcome us home. My eyes welled up with tears, and I couldn't stop sobbing.

I went to the bar for a ginger ale. An older man put his hand on my shoulder and asked if I was OK.

"They didn't do this the last time," I said.

"Vietnam?" he asked. I nodded.

"We apologize," he said in a distinct voice that I will never forget. The sobbing started again.

That night, I felt that a great weight had been lifted from me. Because I was sober, I was there to receive the one thing I'd prayed over for 20 years: I wanted at least one person to welcome a soldier home. So for me, this was a miracle.

I now live in Vancouver, Washington. That backpack they found me with has turned into a house, and walking has turned into a couple of used cars. The feeling of uselessness has turned into a career in nursing, a profession I love. Every day, I see at least one patient who has, or had, a problem with alcohol or drugs.

In almost 21 years of sobriety, I have heard some talk about God's will. For me, it seems that God's will is the result of actions that I take. Also, I have learned not to care too much about what people think of me; it's more important what I think about them. Finally, I didn't know it when that policeman found me, but I have never been alone.

*John T.*
*Vancouver, Washington*

## The Stranger
September 1989

O utside, on the other side of the window, the late August rain came down in a steady northwest mist. The gray day was cold and damp. Inside, the warm air rising from the radiator vent smelled of dust. I had been in treatment for two weeks and increasingly felt I had made a mistake in committing myself to the hospital. It seemed to me that I was very different from the 25 other veterans with whom I was being treated for alcohol and drug addiction.

I caused no trouble, but simply coasted passively through each day, becoming more and more detached from my surroundings. I felt the old familiar feeling of separation as the bell jar descended, shutting out the world. My counselor sensed my withdrawal and confronted me, pressing me for an explanation. I answered that I felt like a fox in a chicken coop. Her pupils opened wide for a moment, and then her whole demeanor became one of defense. I left the interview knowing from her reaction what I had long suspected—that I was different from other men. I also knew that there was something wrong with me, but I did not know what.

I wondered again if all the killing in Vietnam had changed me in some fundamental and irreversible way. I knew I had lost my innocence and my capacity for joy. I knew that the experiences of war had changed me to the point that all of my illusions about society—our myths, our beliefs, our hypocrisies—had been permanently shattered. I suspected also that I had been too long a soldier, too long lived in a state of emergency after emergency, too many times felt the warm blood of others flow out of their bodies while they cried out from the wound that was killing them. I knew from my reading that these were the reasons why I was bored with the experiences of a normal life, why my subconscious was forever unexpectedly throwing up memories of the war, and why I was burdened with guilt and a sense of futurelessness.

I had felt my old familiar depression returning as I left my encounter with the counselor earlier that morning. Now, sitting on the edge of my bed in my room staring out of the window, I told myself that there was nothing to be done, that I might as well stay in the hospital and finish the treatment. I resisted the thought of suicide once again, and told myself that I would embrace it when the time came.

That night I attended the compulsory Monday night Alcoholics Anonymous meeting on the first floor of the old wing of the hospital. As I walked alone to the meeting, I reflected on the fact that I was half finished with the treatment, and that the lectures and films, although interesting, had not touched me. I began to worry about my chances of staying sober once I left treatment. I entered the auditorium and found a seat well in the back—alone. I had been there the week before, sat in much the same seat, and listened to the selfsame drunkalogs. It all seemed so irrelevant, so miserable, so pathetic. I wasn't like that. I slid down in the seat, quit listening, and began to remember other times and places.

I sat like that for the first hour, consciously drifting in and out of my memories, when I began to hear a voice. It was a quiet voice, but it was also profound in tone and strong in its emotional force. It came from deep within the stranger who now stood at the podium. He was a big blond man with huge hands and the face of a policeman—a policeman who, always seeing people at their worst, had lost faith in human beings. He was dressed like an ordinary merchant seaman and spoke with difficulty, his eyes cast down, his manner one of suppressed anger and embarrassment. It was obvious from his speech that he had not been well-educated. He used no philosophical generalizations, employed no humor, told no ego tales. He talked about his life simply and told us about alcohol, how it had defeated and humiliated him, and how at last he had admitted his powerlessness and sought help. He spoke slowly, pausing between statements, staring into the nothingness of the front row as he struggled to master his emotions. Now and then he would stop his narrative, hunch his shoulders forward in response to the pain he so obviously felt, and struggle to gain control of his emotions. When he looked directly at me for the first time, I felt myself blush with a deep sense of shame.

He said, "All of my life I have felt different than other men, but I did not know why. All of my life I have known something was wrong with me, but I did not know what." I could hear my heart beating, and I began to take quiet breaths to get control of my own emotions. The bell jar lifted, and I became acutely aware of every nuance of his speech and manner. His words were at once so personal and so painful that without warning I found myself identifying with his experiences as if they were my own. He said, "Now I know what's wrong with me. I am an alcoholic." He paused again and stared into the space in front of the podium. Then he began to talk about his recovery and about his long road back from the edge of suicide. When he talked about his feelings, he talked about my feelings, about feelings I had! He had never been to war, was not even a veteran. And yet when he talked, he gave voice to my thoughts. He talked about his troubled youth, his depression, his hopelessness, his inability to stick with anything. I had thought myself unique, but here was another like myself—only he had been sober for five years. He thanked us for listening and sat down.

He was not the last speaker. While the others spoke, I kept going over in my mind what the stranger had said. After the meeting ended I went up to where he was sitting. He sat alone in the front row, slumped down in the seat, staring straight ahead, absorbed in his own thoughts. He looked up at me when he sensed my presence, and I could see in his eyes that it had been difficult for him to confess himself to us. His look at me was at once wary and hostile. I knew that look too. Here was a man I had never seen before in my life, and yet I felt I knew him as well as I knew myself. I spoke and said that he had helped me.

At once his manner changed. He jumped out of his seat, smiled broadly, grasped my hand, asked my name and how long I had been in treatment. His hand was calloused and strong. He stood close to me as he asked me about myself. I could smell the clean smell of laundry soap in his cotton clothes. He didn't let go of my hand and laughed when I spoke about myself as if we both shared some kind of secret. Seeing him laugh I realized he was younger than I thought. He must have had some kind of job where he did hard physical labor. He obviously had just showered and shaved before coming to the meeting. Then he let go of my hand, wrapped his big arm around my shoulders, and led me off into a corner of the large room where we were even more alone.

He seemed to know all about me and kept asking questions that caused me to open up to him in a way I later could not understand. He smiled as I talked, locking his eyes into my eyes. As the words rushed out of me, he encouraged me with nods and smiles; sometimes he would laugh out loud and punch me in the arm or thump me on the shoulder. At one point he said, "Why, shoot! You're a stubborn and hard-headed SOB just like me." Without knowing the precise moment when the change occurred, while talking with this stranger, I stopped feeling sorry for myself and for the first time began to hope that maybe I might make it after all.

I don't remember how long we talked. I do know that we were the last ones to leave the auditorium. He walked me to the elevator and said goodbye. I never saw him again. I never even knew his name, but he changed my life. The next day, treatment began to work for me, and in the years that followed I met others like him in various AA meetings throughout the city. One such man became my sponsor and set my steps on the long road back from the brink.

*R. A.*
*Woodinville, Washington*

# Coming Home
October 2017

My company recently hired a military veteran for a second-shift, replacing someone about to retire. The vet was on the job about three months when we got the news that he was found dead in his home. The rumor was that he had shot himself. It was a tragedy and I felt somehow a little guilty. I had met this vet casually in the halls at work. Now, I can only feel his loneliness and wish I had made some connection with him. Being a vet myself, this man's death stirred some feelings, and I started talking to a coworker about coming home from war.

For me, it was Vietnam. For this guy, it was Iraq or Afghanistan, or both. I was treated like a villain when I came home from a war; he was treated like a hero. But no matter. We had the same feelings. Vets are still alone with their thoughts and feelings when they return from war.

I talked to my coworker about some negative things that had happened on my return from Vietnam. I told him about my drinking. I had not been able to stay at the good job I had then, even though my employer thought I was doing well. A manager asked why I was leaving after just a couple months since I had worked there before the war and had done well. How could I tell him that I had to drink or I might kill myself, that drinking was more important to me than the job?

I don't remember what I said to that manager. I know I had no answer for him. Maybe by walking away I saved my own life. I drank until I was in that very dark place that opens doors to unthinkable choices. For me, one of these was the choice to go to AA.

I was very much like this newly hired vet who was now dead. Talking to my coworker reminded me of that. As I spoke of my drinking, he said (not knowing I am in AA), "But you were able to quit." And I said "Not without some help."

I thought about Old Tim who passed away over a decade ago, who is remembered in the AA meeting rooms here for several simple sayings. One of these was, "It's the disease of the lonely."

I was lonely when I came to the rooms. Yes, there were people around me, school buddies, even some who had been in the service. But none had been in the war and no one knew what was going on with me, least of all myself.

That loneliness lifted when I began to identify with AA members and got a sponsor. Now, even after years of sobriety, I still sometimes isolate and don't share my thoughts. I think I'm doing OK, but when I'm not talking on a daily basis the little things begin to build up. Soon, some small irritation becomes a backbreaker and I must get out to an AA meeting to listen and share my thoughts to get back to the lighter side of life.

I have no idea if this newly hired vet was an alcoholic or even drank, but I'm thinking he had "the disease of the lonely," and maybe if he had had some outlet for his feelings, like I have found in AA, he too would still be with us and with his family today.

I am not writing in memory of the vet who shot himself, though. That's someone else's job. I did not know him well enough to tell his story. I am writing about the memories of *this* vet, meaning me. I was lucky enough to find a way to combat loneliness with AA meetings and with the Steps and tools for living.

At a meeting last night, I heard a speaker share that her reactions to life—always at one extreme or the other, overly controlling or submissive—had been a result of injury and wounds from childhood that she had not spoken of, cried about and released. Her controlling and her submissive responses were rooted in these old injuries, and by sharing the old injury, she could set herself free of it. She could be a better-balanced, more mature person, able to treat herself and others with more compassion and respect.

The vet who shot himself brought me back to a place that was uncomfortable. But maybe by feeling that discomfort again, I have been given the opportunity to let go of a little more of it. Maybe I've learned to have a little more compassion for the vet in me and to live the rest of this life with more patience and compassion for others.

*Kurt S.*
*Farmington, Connecticut*

# Incoming!
October 2017

**N**ot only are there lots of atheists with decades of sobriety in AA, there have always been atheists in foxholes.

A graduate of a Christian high school, I enlisted in the Marine Corps at age 19. I had already discovered that the more I studied the scriptures and the more earnestly I prayed, the more I doubted the existence of any kind of God. I've rediscovered this many more times through the years.

Five years into what would become a 25-year career in the Marines, I was diagnosed by a physician as an "acute, chronic alcoholic." A Vietnam veteran with an impeccable service record, I was hospitalized briefly and introduced to AA.

I was happy when they told me at my first meeting that AA is "spiritual, not religious," and "not allied with any sect [or] denomination." But my spirits fell when the meeting began with a prayer, followed by a ritual recitation that invoked the name of God no fewer than six times ("How It Works"). They then closed the meeting by saying the Lord's Prayer.

It was instantly clear to me that AA was a religious cult in denial about being religious. So I didn't come back to any meetings for years. In the meantime, on several occasions I almost died from my alcoholism.

My disease progressed through an additional five years in the Marines. The Commandant of the Marine Corps then ordered me to the National Naval Medical Center at Bethesda, Maryland, for treatment of alcoholism. At least two good things happened to me the second time I was hospitalized.

First, a long-sober Marine master gunnery sergeant who was a counselor at the treatment facility helped square me away on the Higher Power question. He pointed out that all Marines have the same Higher Power—the Commandant of the Marine Corps.

In addition, the master gunny noted that he and I had both been in harm's way earlier in our careers. We talked about a phenomenon with which we were both quite familiar, something known as "esprit de corps." "Esprit" is the French word for "spirit." And "corps" refers to a body of troops, in this case, our Corps of Marines.

We knew from hard experience that when the situation is grave, Marines help each other survive by working together. In fact, another favorite term among Marines, "gung ho," is an ancient Chinese battle cry that means "working together."

The master gunny and I had both been in situations where we and those around us were scared out of our minds. But we knew that when Marines support each other selflessly, we can and do overcome our fear. In doing so, we gain an ability to beat seemingly insurmountable and life-threatening odds.

We knew that the bond Marines feel with each other, especially in combat, is best described as spiritual. This is clearly not a supernatural power, but a deeply human power that has been proven throughout history to play a decisive role in turning potential defeat into victory on the battlefield.

"Esprit de corps is the same kind of spiritual power that AA has," the master gunny explained. "People in AA call this power whatever they want."

The second good thing that happened to me in treatment was that I found my first sponsor. I noticed him at an AA meeting they drove us to in a hospital van one evening. He was the one guy in the room at the end of the meeting whose lips weren't moving when everybody else was holding hands and reciting the Lord's Prayer.

An atheist with 10 years of sobriety at the time, my first sponsor explained to me that even though much of the AA program borrows from religion, AA works just fine anyway, as long as you don't drink, go to lots of meetings and take as many of AA's suggestions as you can stomach.

Working the Twelve suggested Steps to the best of my ability wouldn't kill me, my sponsor said. Even as an atheist, he explained, I could work the Steps exactly the same way everybody else works them—imperfectly and according to my own understanding.

Before my first year in sobriety ended, my career as a Marine rocketed into a new dimension. The Commandant ordered me back to college, where I completed my bachelor's degree. Shortly after my second anniversary in sobriety, people were saluting me and addressing me as "sir."

My attainment of officer rank led to a number of new and exciting assignments all over the world. Each time I moved, I found a new AA sponsor locally and tried to attend 90 meetings in 90 days. I also began sponsoring other men and got involved in AA service work.

During the Persian Gulf War in 1990, I was able to attend a few AA meetings at the Marine headquarters in Dhahran, Saudi Arabia. However, I spent most of my time out in the desert on the front lines, where I enjoyed reading and rereading letters I received from my many AA friends back in the U.S.

For the record, Marines don't have "foxholes." We call them "fighting holes." While under fire during Operation Desert Storm, I observed an important difference between the atheists I knew and others who might be inclined to spend time on their knees praying for divine protection. I found that the atheists could be counted on to do things that are actually useful, like digging better fighting holes.

Some years later, I found myself in Somalia in the midst of a civil war characterized by sectarian violence, famine and human suffering on a Biblical scale. Even though we could find no sign of a "loving God" anywhere in Somalia, I and a few other military personnel formed a group conscience and decided to start holding AA meetings in beautiful downtown Mogadishu.

Our little group opted to meet outdoors in the shade of a tree because of the heat. That turned out to be a mistake. Our first meeting was broken up by sniper fire. Although the sniper was clearly a lousy shot, we decided to change locations.

Our second meeting was broken up by sniper fire too. At that point, we decided to move our meeting indoors behind concrete walls and simply ignore the heat. It was our group's little joke that we closed our meetings "in the usual manner" by all shouting, "Incoming!"

About a year after returning to the U.S., I married a woman I'd met in AA who is also an atheist. We had two children before I retired from the Marines. Today, our kids are grown and doing well.

As of this writing I have 33 years of sobriety in AA and my wife has 26 years. Our lives are as happy, joyous and free as anyone we know in our Fellowship.

But some in AA still "feel sorry" for atheists, just as our co-founder Dr. Bob said he felt about unbelievers in the Big Book. Some too remain convinced that those who say they won't believe are "belligerent" and have a "savage" mind, as cofounder Bill W. asserted in the *Twelve Steps and Twelve Traditions*.

My original atheist AA sponsor, with whom I remain in touch, has 43 years of sobriety in AA and is still clearly a thorn in the side of some of the bleeding deacons in his own home group.

In recent years, I've a played a role in organizing a couple of secular "We Agnostics" meetings of AA in my community. I've also tried to be more vocal at other AA meetings about my lack of belief in any kind of God, especially the miracle-working supernatural being that Bill W. and Dr. Bob believed in.

If AA is to survive and thrive in a world where increasing numbers of people, especially young people, are leaving religious beliefs behind them, as I did, my hope is that we will open the doors of our Fellowship a little wider.

*Eric C.*
*Traverse City, Michigan*

## The Last Thing in His Wallet

June 2015

I came in two weeks after my 21st birthday, and I'm 73 now. I can still remember gulping down a glass of wine when I was 7 and getting that indescribable feeling. My next drink was in high school, seven years later. I blacked out often, but I thought everyone else did too. I joined the U.S. Marine Corps in 1959. After basic training I was given a demanding job and I drank like the rest of the guys. I was soon shipped to Okinawa for a tour, where alcohol was readily available.

While I was there, I started teaching Sunday school class at Kedena Air Base. Once the chaplain of our camp invited me to an officers' meeting about alcoholism in the armed forces and the problems it caused. I thought they had me there to represent the enlisted personnel and give them some advice, but no one asked for it. When he dropped me off that night, the chaplain asked me what we should do about my problem. I had no idea what he was talking about. Within a couple days he had someone take me to an AA meeting. I knew what AA was because a high school classmate told me about her father being in it.

I started going to meetings, carrying all the resentments anyone could hold. Things could've fallen into place for me, but I couldn't let that happen. I have to admit that the meetings sure spoiled my drinking. I thought I'd had remorse before, but nothing like after being introduced to AA.

When I got back to the U.S., I arrived in Barstow, California for duty after three weeks of not drinking. I knew I should look up AA, but I kept saying I'd do it tomorrow. Before I knew it, someone offered me a beer at the club, and I was off. Because I was under 21, I had to do my drinking in the desert by myself. But even when I turned 21, I still found myself drinking alone in the desert.

Then one morning I found myself in a parking lot in bad condition. I wasn't sure what day it was and didn't know if I was on duty or not. All I knew was that I needed to straighten up fast and get back to camp. I went to a restaurant and found a booth in the back to get a cup of coffee and realized my driver's license, military I.D. and liberty card were all missing. The only thing left in my wallet was a Serenity Prayer from a 1960 Grapevine! I then realized that AA was the only thing left for me. I also knew that I didn't want to drink anymore—and that I didn't have to.

I hitched a ride back to camp and threw my dirty clothing in the trash, cleaned up and went back to town to look up AA. I called right away. I didn't wait for tomorrow. A man who answered the phone said he'd pick me up at 7:30. He said his name was Bill.

At the AA meeting, people told stories that paralleled my own life. After it ended, Bill gave me a key to the clubhouse. With the key he gave me permission to go there anytime and read and drink coffee. And while I was there, he said I could dust, clean, straighten up, empty ashtrays and take out the trash.

At a few months sober, I went to San Diego for surgery, and I didn't wait till tomorrow to call AA. I called right away. Jim B. answered, the guy from the "The Vicious Cycle" story in the Big Book. He came to see me that same day. When I was able to go to meetings, he would pick me up. At one meeting, a man who had a number of years said he'd gone back out drinking because he quit going to meetings. Jim looked at me and said, "Remember that!" I met Jim's wife Rosa and spent time drinking coffee with them at their home. What a couple. They told it the way it was.

At 23, I got out of the Marine Corps with two years of sobriety. When I went to hand in my key to the clubhouse, they told me to keep it and remember them. Since then I've been back to Barstow three times in sobriety, twice driving a truck and once on a trip with my wife. I always found AA alive there.

During my time in the program I've gone to two International Conventions: San Diego and San Antonio. I also attended a conference in Rochester, Minnesota, where I met my wife-to-be. We have three daughters who live within 25 miles of us—just another blessing—along with eight grandchildren and one great-grandchild.

I've been able to make meetings from Arizona to Alaska and from California to Maine. During my last years of driving, I spent some time in Aurora, Colorado, and would at times sleep in my truck in the parking lot of the Primary Purpose Group. Someone would knock on my door to wake me up for early morning meetings.

I've found that my length of sobriety isn't as important as today is. The older ones told me that, but it took me time to fully understand it. As I grow older, I find many things they told me have become true. Today is the most important day of my life, and as long as I can remember it, I'll stay sober.

*Louie S.*
*Galesville, Wisconsin*

# The Twelve Steps

1. We admitted we were powerless over alcohol—that our lives had become unmanageable.
2. Came to believe that a Power greater than ourselves could restore us to sanity.
3. Made a decision to turn our will and our lives over to the care of God *as we understood Him.*
4. Made a searching and fearless moral inventory of ourselves.
5. Admitted to God, to ourselves, and to another human being the exact nature of our wrongs.
6. Were entirely ready to have God remove all these defects of character.
7. Humbly asked Him to remove our shortcomings.
8. Made a list of all persons we had harmed, and became willing to make amends to them all.
9. Made direct amends to such people wherever possible, except when to do so would injure them or others.
10. Continued to take personal inventory and when we were wrong promptly admitted it.
11. Sought through prayer and meditation to improve our conscious contact with God *as we understood Him,* praying only for knowledge of His will for us and the power to carry that out.
12. Having had a spiritual awakening as the result of these steps,  we tried to carry this message to alcoholics, and to practice these principles in all our affairs.

# The Twelve Traditions

1. Our common welfare should come first; personal recovery depends upon A.A. unity.
2. For our group purpose there is but one ultimate authority—a loving God as He may express Himself in our group conscience. Our leaders are but trusted servants; they do not govern.
3. The only requirement for A.A. membership is a desire to stop drinking.
4. Each group should be autonomous except in matters affecting other groups or A.A. as a whole.
5. Each group has but one primary purpose—to carry its message to the alcoholic who still suffers.
6. An A.A. group ought never endorse, finance or lend the A.A. name to any related facility or outside enterprise, lest problems of money, property and prestige divert us from our primary purpose.
7. Every A.A. group ought to be fully self-supporting, declining outside contributions.
8. Alcoholics Anonymous should remain forever nonprofessional, but our service centers may employ special workers.
9. A.A., as such, ought never be organized; but we may create service boards or committees directly responsible to those they serve.
10. Alcoholics Anonymous has no opinion on outside issues; hence the A.A. name ought never be drawn into public controversy.
11. Our public relations policy is based on attraction rather than promotion; we need always maintain personal anonymity at the level of press, radio and films.
12. Anonymity is the spiritual foundation of all our traditions, ever reminding us to place principles before personalities.

## AA Grapevine

AA Grapevine is AA's international monthly journal, published continuously since its first issue in June 1944. The AA pamphlet on AA Grapevine describes its scope and purpose this way: "As an integral part of Alcoholics Anonymous since 1944, the Grapevine publishes articles that reflect the full diversity of experience and thought found within the A.A. Fellowship, as does La Viña, the bimonthly Spanish-language magazine, first published in 1996. No one viewpoint or philosophy dominates their pages, and in determining content, the editorial staff relies on the principles of the Twelve Traditions."

In addition to magazines, AA Grapevine, Inc. also produces an app, books, eBooks, audiobooks, and other items. It also offers a Grapevine Online subscription, which includes: new stories weekly, AudioGrapevine (the audio version of the magazine), the Grapevine Story Archive and the current issue of Grapevine and La Viña in HTML format. For more information on AA Grapevine, or to subscribe to any of these, please visit the magazine's website at aagrapevine.org or write to:

AA Grapevine, Inc.
475 Riverside Drive
New York, NY 10115

## Alcoholics Anonymous

AA's program of recovery is fully set forth in its basic text, *Alcoholics Anonymous* (commonly known as the Big Book), now in its Fourth Edition, as well as in *Twelve Steps and Twelve Traditions*, *Living Sober*, and other books. Information on AA can also be found on AA's website at www.aa.org, or by writing to:

Alcoholics Anonymous
Box 459
Grand Central Station
New York, NY 10163

For local resources, check your local telephone directory under "Alcoholics Anonymous." Four pamphlets, "This is A.A.," "Is A.A. For You?," "44 Questions," and "A Newcomer Asks" are also available from AA.